AND ON THIS ROCK

AND ON THIS ROCK

The Witness of One Land and Two Covenants

Second Edition, Revised and Enlarged

Stanley L. Jaki

TRINITY COMMUNICATIONS
MANASSAS, VIRGINIA

Second Edition

©Trinity Communications 1987

ISBN 0-937495-09-3, paper
    0-937495-10-7, cloth

Original edition published in 1978 by Ave Maria Press

Table of Contents

Preface   5

Introduction   7

I. The Scene of the Rock   15

II. God the Rock   55

III. A Man Called Rock   71

IV. The Shadow of the Rock   93

V. Divine Origin of the Papacy   106

Epilogue   128

Preface to the New Edition

This book was researched, written, and published in an agonizing period of the Roman Catholic Church's recent history. By the early 1970s it was an open secret that Pope Paul VI had become deeply discouraged by the direction in which the "spirit" of Vatican II was luring some bishops, many priests, and countless faithful. Respect for papal authority sank to a far lower point in many Catholic circles than it did at any time during the previous four or five generations. The dramatic ascendency of respect, which was secured to the papacy by the extraordinary figure of John Paul II, did not mean a similar rise of respect for papal authority. Many of those "theologians" who in the 1970s clamored for a "democratic" church are still around and busy with their anti-papal agenda. To be sure, their voice is not so voluble. If they still sound occasionally in decibels, they do so mostly in desperation. Their rout is on, although not without some ghastly decay and sheer tragedies coming to full light.

As with tragedies in general, here too the act of dénouement may be the most shocking but not necessarily the most deplorable part of a dispiriting story. On seeing, say, a talented young Jesuit, winner of several Emmy awards, "resign" in protest against papal authority, one may feel one's heart break. But what really should cast a pallor over one's mind is the "encouragement" that helped his and many similar tragedies. Those mindful of the principle that actual failing is less a crime than a thematic conditioning for it, will know what to think of the hubris that may lurk behind the guideline given by a Jesuit provincial: "The Jesuits have always been on the cutting edge and the Pope does not expect us to repeat his mind: he expects us to challenge it."

Nothing is so sad in the actual tensions within the Church than the still unrepentant attitude of a goodly segment of the Society of Jesus. Although the chief distinction there is the admittance to solemn vows, of which the fourth is a pledge of loyalty to the pope, many Jesuits pride themselves in resisting the pope and in instilling in others an attitude of defiance toward him.

This was hardly the contradiction foreseen by the Cardinal Archbishop of Cracow as he preached to Paul VI and his household a retreat on "the sign of contradiction." But after eight years in the chair of Peter, John Paul II felt it imperative to diagnose a festering situation with plain reference to the devil being loose inside the Church. The actual storm around the Rock is indeed so skillfully orchestrated from within that it is not difficult to see there the work of one who prefers to appear as the angel of light. His chief aim is to spread the perception that the Rock is but a time-conditioned result, however useful until recently, and that it can safely be downgraded with the advent of these "progressive" times of ours. It is therefore all the more timely to re-articulate and ponder the divine truth that the Rock, or Peter, has an endurance of which the end of all times is the only true measure.

Introduction

In the Spring of 1973 two postcards came to me from a great distance. They were sent by friends, a Nobel-laureate physicist and his wife. I had known them for years but this was the first time that they expressed in this way their feelings for me. One postcard would have been a touching gesture, but now two came within two weeks.

My friends were on their first visit to Israel and, I presume, they thought it natural to send a greeting from there to a friend who happened to be a Roman Catholic priest. Not being Catholics, not even members of any church, although Christians in a broader sense, they certainly showed their thoughtfulness by choosing for the first postcard one which recorded Pope Paul's historic visit to the Holy Land. The postcard somehow disappeared in my piles of notes, but the scene it portrayed did not vanish from my memory. The focus of the scene was the white-robed pope in a crimson red cloak kneeling in prayer on a grey stone pavement. Around him were columns supporting Gothic arches, a structure built by the Crusaders on the traditional spot of the Last Supper.

For non-Catholics to send this particular card to a priest friend was understandable enough. But the choice of the second card was not so easy to explain. It showed some ruins around Banias, a place known in Roman times as Caesarea Philippi. The

Holy Land contains much beautiful scenery and many impressive ruins—all of which are more strongly promoted for tourists than Banias. In all likelihood my friends did not suspect that Christ uttered some words there. Therefore it could hardly occur to them that those words addressed to Peter, "You are 'Rock,' and on this rock I will build my church," are of primary importance for Roman Catholics.

Much less could my friends suspect the impact the postcard was to have on me. The first book I wrote was a survey of new trends on the idea and reality of the Church—in short, ecclesiology. The book, *Les tendances nouvelles de l'ecclésiologie*, was first published in 1957, and again in 1963 during Vatican II.[1] Word about it was carried to countless non-theologians through Professor Küng's *The Church* where the first book he refers to is my *Tendances,* cited because of its "valuable contributions to the history of ecclesiology."[2] He should have perhaps advised his readers that I saw the "trends" in a light quite different from his. In my *Tendances* the present Church, resting on the rock which is Peter living in his successors, serves as the explanation of a theological past, however recent or remote. In his *Church,* dedicated to Dr. Michael Ramsey, Archbishop of Canterbury, a diffusely living Christendom is measured against a rather abstract conceptual scheme. It is abstract in the sense that it fails to fit any concrete phase of the historic Church, and leaves him, as was noted by a leading Anglican theologian, "in much the same quandary as the sixteenth-century reformers." The latter "were at the mercy of the literal text [of the New Testament] as understood by their several minds under the illumination of the inner light, while he [Küng] is at the mercy of contemporary biblical scholarship."[3]

By 1967, when Küng's *Church* was published, I had long ceased to be an active theologian. Complications due to a tonsillectomy forced me to give up teaching theology in 1954. It was, however, interest in theology that led me first into the deep waters of modern physics, and from there to the even deeper currents of the history and philosophy of science. The work I had done in that field was dedicated to the defense of certain theses—the existence of mind as distinct from matter; the fundamental importance for scientific method of an epistemology embodied in the classical proofs of the existence of God; the limited validity or relevance of exact science or physics; the crucial importance of Christian belief in creation for the unique rise of science—theses which, like my ecclesiological thesis, could make me appear an anachronism in the eyes of many theologians who "earned their wings" from the 1960's on. One of these, whom I encountered, was an admirer of second-century Gnostics and frowned on St. Irenaeus' massive unmasking of them.[4] He was also an advocate of cremation without even keeping the ashes in a small urn. He gave me a condescending smile on hearing my views on the brain-mind relationship which I had developed with an eye on "thinking machines," that is, computers. His smile turned into a sudden embarrassment when I asked him in return: "Is there still going to be a Father Joseph Smith (the name is fictitious) after his ashes have been duly sprinkled on the flower beds of the monastery garden?" "I have not given much thought to that," was his subdued answer.

Such lack of concern about the consequences of tampering with fundamental theological as well as philosophical tenets is the most dangerous phenomenon in the Church today. True, even some of the unwary are now beginning to see deadly traps opening wide as they find the divinity of Christ being openly called into doubt, and not rarely by those who have already done their "critical" work on the Church.[5] It takes no theological expertise to suspect that once Christ is reduced to the rank of mere man, however exalted, he will speak with no more authority than the "authoritative" illusion which is the lot of all self-assertive men. Any slighting of the divine authority of Christ can only divest Christ of himself, a logic easily seen by the most common of the faithful, precisely because they have all too often a much larger measure of common sense than do some uncommonly famous theological writers.

What the ordinary faithful will not see with the same immediacy is the logic which connects one's attitude to Christ's authority with one's attitude to ecclesiastical authority. He clearly established this authority when he decreed that faith, the road to salvation, ought to be a response to the words of those whom he had endowed with an appallingly large measure of authority. He promised them his unrestricted support from heaven for *whatever* they would loose or bind on earth.

From the late 1960's on, many thoughtful minds in the Church agonized over the inevitable unfolding of the logic whereby some tried to dissociate those two authorities. I was in such a state of mind when those two postcards arrived. The one showing the pope kneeling on the floor of the Cenacle reminded me of the fact that he was kneeling perhaps on the very spot where once Christ knelt as he washed the feet of the Twelve and reminded them of his own authority. Clearly, by enjoining on them the duty of washing the feet of those entrusted to them he did not intend to diminish the authority he had already conferred upon them.

The other postcard showed, together with some ruins, a most striking scene—a huge wall of bare rock—around Caesarea Philippi where the greatest possible authority was ever given to mere man. For not only are the keys to open and to close a symbol of authority. The rock or foundation, which Simon, son of Jonah, was solemnly declared, is also symbolic of authority. Since faith or salvation is a response to authoritative preaching of truth, authority is but another aspect of a rock foundation. Men are transformed into living stones by responding to such preaching, and thus built into the everlasting edifice—the Church of the living God.

It could only mean agony to see so many stones slowly detaching themselves from that edifice as they were swayed by the voices of theologians who in the most authoritative tone taught them how to flout authority. That they were not taught theology but only to question authority was made all too evident by book titles such as *Infallible?*[6], a title most conspicuous by its question mark. It questioned not so much infallibility as theology itself. The reason for this lies in the fact that theology is a science. Yet theology can only be a science if it is a consistent discourse, of which, however, there is little in that book. Its author urged, four years after Vatican II, the correcting of Vatican I not in the light of Vatican II but "in the light of the Gospel."[7] Curiously, that light did not include a new and careful look at those words which, according to the Gospel, Christ addressed to Peter "in the neighborhood of Caesarea Philippi." By some infallibly revealing tactic those words of Christ were merely referred to in that 250-page book devoted to casting doubt on the infallibility of Peter's successors.[8] Clearly, Küng's slighting of those words could only be taken as a sign of an infallible conclusion, reached by a fallible theologian, that those words offer no support whatever on behalf of the pope's infallibility.

A book on infallibility, in which the name Caesarea Philippi does not occur even once, should seem a most fallible and most un-Gospel-like enterprise even on a cursory look. The truth of this was forcefully suggested to me by what I saw on the second postcard. The same truth loomed enormous when, prompted by that postcard, I finally travelled to Caesarea Philippi. Unlike most other pilgrims to the Holy Land I reached that spot on a first and very brief visit there. Anticipation of a great find kept me in the dark about the impracticability of my plans. When a scientific conference in Athens in 1974 brought me reasonably close to the Holy Land, I did not realize that, if one had only four days to see something of that land, Caesarea Philippi could be farther from Jerusalem than Jerusalem is from Athens. Yet, although I arrived in Jerusalem without any guidance from tourist or pilgrimage agencies, a series of most lucky coincidences (Providence, I humbly believe) directed my steps from the very start toward my chief target. The party which organized the one-day trip to Galilee, of which I became a part by "sheer-luck," wanted to go no farther than the Golan Heights. Even when, at my begging, the driver was told to take us as far north as Banias (a detour of at least three hours from the original itinerary) my companions, all Christians, were surprised to hear from me that Christ and Church had something to do with Banias, that is, Caesarea Philippi.

Through Providence again (acting this time through the generosity of a convert to Catholicism who wants to remain anonymous) I was back in Banias two years later not only with rolls of film but also with a full record of all references in the Old Testament to the Rock which is God. That such a record had previously been compiled—by first-rate biblical scholars—only in skeletal manner, mostly in the form of a generic statement followed by an always lifeless row of numbers indicating chapter and verse,[9] puzzled me in no small measure. I wondered if by remaining a professional theologian my mental eyes had not remained conditioned to that professionally facile handling of most weighty passages. Fortunately, I consulted the theological and biblical literature on the topic of rock only after the core of this essay had been worked out. It was due to my pondering on those passages that the postcard from Caesarea Philippi and my visits there had an impact on me which most scholars visiting there apparently did not experience. If they did, they certainly failed to communicate it in writing.

I cannot help feeling that a careful consideration of the breadth and width, to say nothing of the depth, of those Old Testament texts would have long ago imposed the recognition of a specific scene at Caesarea Philippi as the very setting in which a man was declared to be Rock or Peter by no less an authority than the Son of God. That recognition could in turn have greatly helped some able minds to put not a question mark but a mark of exclamation after the word *infallible*. That comprises the personal background of this essay. Whatever there is still personal in it is told in an impersonal manner so that what is the finding of one, may all the more readily become the enrichment of many. They may, however, notice that documentation and scholarly details given in the Notes are not necessarily the most impersonal part of any book.

NOTES

[1]Rome: Casa Editrice Herder. The work is an enlarged form of my doctoral dissertation presented in 1950 at the Istituto Pontificio di San Anselmo, Rome.

[2]See, Küng, *The Church* (New York: Sheed and Ward, 1967), p. 6.

[3]E.L. Mascall in *The Tablet,* Jan. 27, 1968 (vol. 222, no. 6662), p. 77.

[4]The unmasking is Irenaeus' *Adversus haereses,* readily available in English translation (*Against the Heresies*) in the Ante-Nicene Library. Those able to see the philosophical and theological subjectivism lurking behind the often bizarre but invariably syncretistic creeds which are Irenaeus' target, will find in his book a prophetic warning against that gnosticism which in our times often parades in the guise of "progressive" theology. This point was made with gentle incisiveness by R. Graber (Bishop of Regensburg) in his *Athanasius and the Church of Our Time on the 1600th Anniversary of His Death,* translated from the German by Susan Johnson (Gerrards Cross, U.K.: Van Duren, 1974).

[5]There is indeed a straight road of logic from Küng's *Structures of the Church,* translated from the German by S. Attanasio (New York: T. Nelson, 1964) to his *On Being a Christian,* translated from the German by E. Quinn (Garden City, N.Y.: Doubleday, 1976). The latter work prompted Joseph Cardinal Höffner, chairman of the German bishops' conference, to request Küng's answer to the question: "Is Jesus Christ the pre-existing, eternal Son of God, one in being with the Father?", a question to which Küng refused to give an unequivocal answer. See *Time,* Feb. 27, 1978, p. 44. (His refusal ultimately led to the Vatican's declaration that he was no longer a Catholic theologian.) The logic in question consists in choosing for one's starting point not the actual living Church but a hypothetical construct taken for the primitive Church. The result reminds one of that explorer who a century or so ago took a pool in south-central Africa for the source of the Congo and ended up on the Nile.

[6]Küng's book, *Infallible? An Inquiry,* translated from the German

by E. Quinn (Garden City, N.Y.: Doubleday, 1971), was first published in 1970.

[7]Since that "light of the Gospel" is severed in Küng's book from the actual, living Church, it makes him oblivious to that light which Jesus provided in the Gospel by his warning concerning the splinter in the eyes of others and the beam in one's own eyes. Whereas Küng chastised the living pope in the light of a hypothetical "model pope" imbued solely with pastoral sensitivity and humility, he did not expect the same virtues to animate the "model theologian." That Küng's "light of the Gospel" is rather un-Gospel-like can also be seen from the fact that his "model-shepherd" is without a shepherd's staff, that is, without the power to lay down rules for some patently unruly sheep.

[8]See *Infallible? An Inquiry*, pp. 95, 97, 109-111.

[9]That such rows of numbers do not, as a rule, prompt most readers (including students of theology) to look up the passages in the Bible, prompted the eminent theologian, M. Schmaus, to have most scriptural references quoted in full in his monumental *Katholische Dogmatik*. See the preface to the first edition (1937), p. x.

I. The Scene of the Rock

The Gospel of Saint John, which in more than one sense is a completion of the four Gospels, comes to a close with a charming exaggeration. No one has ever taken but for hyperbole St. John's remark that if all Jesus said and did were written down, the world would not be large enough to contain the books. Whatever the number of books that could be filled with the words and deeds of Jesus, a fair account of all the places he visited could possibly be given in a few volumes. One slender volume would in fact be enough to list and describe briefly the places we actually know he stayed or passed through.

One of these places is the neighborhood of Caesarea Philippi, conspicuously mentioned by Matthew and conspicuously slighted by biblical scholars. Such is a curious slighting if one recalls that in the neighborhood of Caesarea Philippi Jesus uttered a phrase which, even disregarding its content, is by its form one of the most conspicuous among his always momentous declarations.

While the declaration—"I for my part declare to you, you are Rock and on this rock I will build my church and the jaws of death shall not prevail against it" (Mt. 16:16)—is all too well known, there has developed no broad awareness of the "neighborhood of Caesarea Philippi."

Since a neighborhood can be fairly large, identifying a particular section in it may seem inherently conjectural. Yet would any doubt linger, say, about the spot where John the Baptizer greeted Jesus on the bank of the Jordan, if nature had marked that spot as conspicuously as is marked a spot in the neighborhood of Caesarea Philippi? This marker is the precipitous southern end of one of the foothills of Mount Hermon forming a wall of bare rock about 200 feet high and 500 feet wide. Immediately in front of that wall of rock, there is today a set of rectangular basins which collect the waters from the springs of one of the three upper branches of the Jordan. The other two branches have their sources a dozen or so miles to the west and join the eastern branch at about five miles below Banias, an Arab village in complete ruins since the war of 1967.

Banias is the Arabic variant of Panias, a place of Pan's cult in classical antiquity. This is one of the reasons why the Jordan's source at Banias, a source less abundant in water than the two other sources to the west, is far more abundant in historical significance. The source at Banias also excels the other two in natural beauty. This fact was undoubtedly a chief reason why Philip, the tetrarch, chose that site for Caesarea Philippi, a city he built in honor of Caesar Augustus. The city (now barely a ruin) lay between that wall of rock and a set of beautiful cascades which the eastern branch of the Jordan produces as it breaks through a plateau toward the plains of northern Galilee.

The area of Panias was noted principally for its beauty by Josephus, the famed Jewish historian, while the cult of Pan was still flourishing there and Caesarea Philippi had not yet lost any of its splendor. Josephus obviously spoke through first hand experience as he described Panias. Although a chief spokesman of submission to Rome, Josephus, when hardly thirty, was forced to lead the hopeless insurrection which took place in Galilee against the Romans in 66 A.D. As a prisoner he told Vespasian, leader of the Roman legions holding Galilee, that he (Vespasian) would one day become Caesar. After Jerusalem's

View of the wall of rock from a quarter of a mile
(photograph by the author, 1976)

Ruins of walls of Caesarea Philippi
(photograph by the author, 1976)

destruction, Vespasian, already Caesar, recalled the strange prophecy and not only set Josephus free, but also gave him a large estate in his homeland. Thus Josephus had further and ample opportunity to study the chain of events on the spot that led to the complete subjugation of the Jews and to their forced dispersion throughout the Roman empire.

In that chain, events connected with Panias played only a small role, but a sufficiently characteristic one to draw Josephus' attention to it. In *The Jewish War,* which Josephus wrote toward the end of Vespasian's reign (69-79), Josephus takes up the description of Panias almost at the outset of his story, namely, with Herod's time. Herod, as Josephus notes, was eager to please the Jews (whom he ruled with the support of the Romans), as well as the Romans. He earned Jewish gratitude by enormously enlarging the Temple precincts of Jerusalem. When Rome enlarged Herod's fiefdom in return for his services, Herod, so goes Josephus' narration, reciprocated by building, in honor of Caesar Augustus, "a temple of white marble near the sources of the Jordan, at a place called Paneion."

Josephus continues: "At this spot a mountain rears its summit to an immense height aloft; at the base of the cliff is an opening into an overgrown cavern; within this, plunging down to an immeasurable depth, is a yawning chasm, enclosing a volume of still water, the bottom of which no sounding line has been found long enough to reach. Outside and from beneath the cavern well up the springs from which, as some think, the Jordan takes its rise."[1] In the same breath Josephus warns his reader that the truth about the sources of the Jordan would be revealed later in his book.

The opportunity for this came as Josephus described the pursuit by Titus, Vespasian's son, of defeated Jewish warriors toward the headwaters of the Jordan. After noting that Philip, the tetrarch, proved that the Jordan's true origin was not at Paneion (Panias) but in a pool called Phiale[2] from which the water passed underground to Panias, Josephus notes: "The natu-

ral beauties of Paneion have been enhanced by royal munifi-
cence, the place having been embellished by Agrippa at great
expense. After issuing from this grotto the Jordan, whose course
is now visible, intersects the marshes and lagoons . . . then tra-
verses another hundred and twenty furlongs, and . . . cuts across
the Lake of Gennesar."[3]

In Josephus' *Jewish Antiquities*, completed toward the end
of his life (c. 95 A.D.), Panias is given an even more graphic account in connection with Caesar Augustus' visit in Syria in 20
A.D. Herod was there to greet him and "after escorting Augustus to the sea, he erected to him a very beautiful temple of
white stone in the territory of Zenodorus, near the place called
Paneion. In the mountains here there is a beautiful cave, and
below it the earth slopes steeply to a precipitous and inaccessi-
ble depth, which is filled with still water, while above it is a
very high mountain. Below the cave rise the sources of the river
Jordan. It was this most celebrated place that Herod further
adorned with the temple which he consecrated to Caesar."[4] At
the very end of his *Antiquities* Josephus also notes that Caesarea
Philippi was renamed Neronias by Agrippa.[5]

Behind this brief reference by Josephus to a new name for
Caesarea Philippi, lay details worthy of the power of darkness.
Such details include Agrippa's sheer opportunism (also evident
in his brushing off Paul when his preaching became too dis-
turbing to bear); the diabolical mores of Nero, who killed his
wife Poppaea by kicking her in the belly and then declaring her
a goddess; and in the cunning of Josephus. When visiting in
Rome shortly before that uprising, he endeared himself first to
Poppaea and then to Nero, through the good services of
Alytirus, a Jewish actor in Rome and a favorite of Poppaea.

Such are then the main details attested to by Josephus, one
of the great writers of antiquity, about Caesarea Philippi: a
splendid pagan city lying in clear sight of a huge wall of rock.
At the top of that wall there glitters the white marble of a temple dedicated to Caesar. At its bottom there is an outwardly

idyllic sanctuary of Pan. Immediately to the left of that sanctuary there is a fathomless cavity full of water, one of the three sources of the Jordan.

All these details were brought within the ken of those countless theologians who in modern times could read the works of Josephus in ever improved translations.[6] The number of editions in which those translations have been brought out for the past two centuries would make a long list. Yet prior to the turn of this century, no list could be made of theologians who would have recognized the similarities between the scene Josephus depicted of Caesarea Philippi and the scene Matthew presents in his Gospel.

Of course, Josephus cannot be blamed for not recalling either Matthew or Peter, let alone Jesus, in that context. Before he was nineteen, Josephus had tried membership in the three main Jewish sects—Sadducees, Essenes, and Pharisees—finally casting his lot with the Pharisees. His dealings with the Romans showed, however, his turning toward a more liberal observance. Therefore Josephus could become liberal to the extent of mentioning Jesus twice, though obliquely, in his voluminous writings,[7] a liberal departure from the Pharisaic verdict of turning Jesus, by systematic silence, into a nonentity.

Concerning Caesarea Philippi, Christian theologians showed an almost complete silence long after the testimony of Josephus began to be strengthened from the early 19th century on by the accounts of explorers of the Holy Land. One of the first of them was John Lewis Burckhardt, a bold traveler who died in 1817 at the age of thirty-three after searching for the source of the Blue Nile. His *Travels in Syria and in the Holy Land* was published only posthumously in 1822,[8] but its importance was immediately recognized when a German translation was published the following year.[9]

The *Travels in Syria and the Holy Land* was full of minute details. However, one detail, a drawing by Burckhardt of the niches of Pan's sanctuary at Banias, was anything but minute.

One of the relatively few drawings in a vast book of 649 quarto pages, it shows the relative size and position of the niches with fair accuracy, but it fails to indicate their smallness with respect to the height of the wall of rock. The chief niche, or the sanctuary itself, is an apse-like cave carved into that wall of rock. It is about twelve feet high and slightly more in depth and width.

Burckhardt's drawing of Pan's sanctuary
(from *Travels in Syria*, p. 38)

The back wall of that sanctuary is broken up at its center by a niche about four feet high and two feet wide. It was most likely occupied by a statue of Pan, as were the three other niches, similar in size but distinctly more ornate, carved, outside that sanctuary, into the wall of rock. One of them is right above the entrance of the sanctuary. The two others are to its right. Of these two the one closer to the sanctuary is about 6 feet from the ground and about 20 feet from the sanctuary itself. The other is 12 feet further to the right and sinks partly into the ground. Burckhardt also deciphered one inscription and mentioned the remains of ancient walls and "quantities of stones and architectural fragments scattered about." He also saw "an entire column of small dimensions."[10]

What Burckhardt failed to mention was a huge irregular cavity to the left of the sanctuary as one faces it.[11] That cavity, which in Josephus' time contained that unfathomable pool, became at a later time, obviously through an earthquake, filled with debris so that the water had to seek an outlet about 50 feet below. But the frontal opening of that cavity, much larger than the sanctuary, remained unobstructed. Its darkness and size form a stark contrast with the clear pools of fresh water below it.[12] That this grim dark opening, easily resembling a dreadful jaw, and the huge wall of rock rising above it could have been the backdrop of a New Testament story told by Matthew about Jesus and Peter, wholly escaped Burckhardt.

The French scholar, Victor Guerin, in his massive geographic, historical and archaeological description of Palestine published in 1880, offered a far superior description of Banias than Burckhardt.[13] Guerin not only quoted in full the relevant passages from Josephus, but gave the texts of inscriptions on the marble plaques decorating the niches.

One inscription under the niche located above the sanctuary states that "this goddess was consecrated to the divine Pan, lover of Echo, by Victor, a priest, son of Lysimachus." The first words of the inscription to the left of the niche located on the far right, state: "To Pan and the nymphs."[14] The rest is undecipherable. The inscription below the niche in the middle tells about the priest of Pan, Valerius, who expiated Pan's ire by making him an offering and consecrating the niche to him, doing so in order to obtain the favor of the emperor.

Guerin also mentioned that many coins referring to Pan had been found in the locality. His source was a scholarly work on the numismatics of the Holy Land published in 1874 by F. de Saulcy, a member of the French Academy.[15] A dozen or so coins show Pan playing the syrinx,[16] and several others show various emperors. One shows Poppaea herself in the entrance of a temple, possibly the one at the top of the huge wall of rock, dedicated to Augustus. Other coins show a naked Jupiter, a possible indication that although the temple was dedicated to Augustus, the statue of Jupiter was its main decor. On one coin the locality is called Caesarea Panias. Equally telling are two coins in which Pan is shown playing the syrinx within that sanctuary.

It was not the purpose of Guerin's work to intimate anything of what went on within that sanctuary or in its idyllic vicinity. To suspect some details one need not make a special study of Pan's cult. It is enough to recall that the cult, which originated in Arcadia half a millennium or so before Christ, was a celebration of fertility. That the celebration readily took on forms of plain orgy is suggested by Pan's most characteristic features: a head decorated with horns, a leery and lustful smile, and the prancing legs of a goat.

The name Pan, a contraction from *Paon*, gave origin to the

Pan's cult   Pan's pipe (syrinx) and
                    the temple of Jupiter
Coins found at Caesarea Philippi
(from *Numismatique de la Terre Sainte,* Planche XVIII)

Pan's sanctuary
(photograph by the author, 1976)

Pan's sanctuary
(photograph by the author, 1976)

Inscription to the left of the lowest niche starting with
PANITEKAINYMPHAIS, to Pan and the nymphs.
(photograph by the author, 1976)

word panic, which may have first referred to the stampeding of a herd.[17] Its further meaning as human fright was a logical outgrowth of the unbridled lust that made Pan's sanctuary first an alluring and then a frightening experience to many. This is to be kept in mind when reading Socrates' prayer, "Oh dear Pan . . . grant me inner beauty of soul," about which a perceptive student of Greek cults had already warned: "There is no Greek cult so primitive and rustic but what some tolerant philosopher could infuse ethical thought into it."[18]

Guerin should have remarked that Caesarea Philippi was the scene of a declaration of conflict between two very different ethics when he briefly noted,[19] following his array of evidence of the existence of Pan's cult there, the connection of the area with the Gospel of Matthew. But he merely quoted the question of Jesus: "Who do people say that the Son of Man is?" Guerin did not so much as hint at Peter's response, let alone the reply of Jesus to Peter's confession of faith.

Possibly, Guerin thought that his detailed account of Panias, and his recall of Jesus' question, would naturally invite his readers to connect the huge rock housing Pan's sanctuary with the Rock Jesus referred to in replying to Peter. That the connection might have been made rather naturally became evident in a spectacular way in 1880, the very year of the publication of Guerin's work. Spectacular indeed was the richness of illustrations in *Picturesque Palestine, Sinai and Egypt*,[20] as was its wealth of information. To produce such a work, its editor, Charles William Wilson, a prominent explorer of the Near East, clearly had to be "assisted by the most prominent Palestine explorers," as stated on the title page.

The four quarto volumes of *Picturesque Palestine* were the fruit of an enterprise sponsored by the Palestine Exploration Fund (London) and put into action by Wilson himself in 1864. Wilson, a captain in the British army corps of engineers and already well known for his part in fixing the boundary line between the United States and British Columbia, volunteered to do the topographical survey of Jerusalem and vicinity. The winter of 1868-69 found him surveying the Sinai peninsula. Once more he returned to London with a wealth of information which, in 1874, earned him fellowship in the Royal Society.[21]

Among Wilson's explorer-collaborators was the Reverend Selah Merrill, a Yale graduate and Congregationalist Civil War chaplain from Massachusetts. In 1873 Merrill went to Palestine as a member of an expedition sponsored by the American Palestine Exploration Society. Its purpose was to do east of the Jordan what the British Palestine Exploration aimed at accomplishing in the Holy Land proper. In 1876-77, during his third trip to Palestine, Merrill headed the expedition, which became a great success. He was then engaged by Wilson to contribute to *Picturesque Palestine* the text of four chapters dealing with the area from Galilee to Mount Hermon. One chapter was entitled "Caesarea Philippi and the Highlands of Galilee."[22]

As a theologian and archaeologist, Merrill had not only a mastery of historical and literary data, but also a keen sensitivity for the peculiarities of the landscape. His description of the village of Banias as it existed in the 1870's, and of its inhabitants' manners, was as graphic as the drawings of Harry Finn and J.D. Woodward. These were undoubtedly the chief reasons for a recent reprinting of a small part of *Picturesque Palestine*, a reprint containing Merrill's chapter on Caesarea Philippi.[23]

Merrill was astonished to see the poverty of the people of Banias, although theirs was an area exceptionally rich in water and vegetation. He found houses built everywhere on old ruins and noticed that above their flat roofs there were "temporary lodging places . . . built of reeds and boughs. They are raised a few feet above the roofs, and the inhabitants climb into them and sleep. These booths are cooler than the rooms below, and besides, in this way the people avoid the scorpions which infest these old ruins."[24]

Far more important than such details was for Merrill a "bold cliff of limestone not far from one hundred feet high," at a short distance to the northeast of the village, a view which was illustrated by a full quarto page drawing. "At its base," Merrill continued, "is a large cave, of which the mouth is obstructed by immense blocks of stone that have fallen from above. What its original shape or dimensions were cannot now be told, for earthquakes, judging by the fallen rocks, have entirely changed the face of the cliff immediately above the cave. From underneath these great stones issue the copious streams which have caused the spot to be named Fountain of the Jordan. . . . The cave and fountain must have been much more extensive in former times than at present, for the place was early chosen as a sanctuary, and Herod the Great, in honour of Augustus, built there a splendid temple of white marble."[25]

After quoting Josephus concerning the origin of the Jordan, Merrill turned his attention to the scene immediately next to that cave, a scene made up of a set of niches carved into the cliff, rendering a beautiful drawing of it. He also noted that the inscriptions of the niches attested to Pan's cult there, taking the view that they had probably been executed in the years following the reign of Herod the Great.

The next item in Merrill's narrative was a recount of various rulers of Caesarea Philippi in antiquity. The last local ruler Merrill mentions was Agrippa II, who, according to Josephus,[26] invited Vespasian to Caesarea Philippi and entertained him and his troops lavishly for several weeks in 67 A.D., or shortly after the subjugation of Galilee. Three years later, Titus, the conqueror of Jerusalem, was entertained by Agrippa in Caesarea Philippi in a truly Roman manner. As reported in Josephus' *Jewish War*,[27] many of the Jewish prisoners of war were thrown into the circus of Caesarea Philippi, taking part in life-to-death struggles with wild beasts, or like gladiators, with one another.

Merrill also reported that the extant coins from Panias covered a period of almost three centuries[28] and gave some details similar to those already listed by Guerin in a much more

The wall of rock and the source of the Jordan
(from *Picturesque Palestine*, vol. I, p. 348)

Pan's sanctuary
(from *Picturesque Palestine*, vol. I, p. 349)

meticulous manner. In recalling that Caesarea Philippi was the seat of a bishop in the fourth century, Merrill did not mention a detail first reported in the *Church History* of Eusebius (c. 263-339), a native of Palestine, and a bishop of the other Caesarea south of Mount Carmel on the shore of the Mediterranean. According to Eusebius, the woman, whom Christ cured of her continual hemorrhage (Mt 9:20), was from Caesarea Philippi and out of gratitude she had erected a statue in Christ's honor in front of her house.[29]

Merrill's omission of this detail should not suggest that Christ had not been very much in his mind as he explored Palestine. Indeed he wrote: "Caesarea Philippi has special claims upon our attention from the fact that it was visited by our Lord."[30] That the transfiguration of Christ may have taken place in that general area was rather probable for Merrill, who together with many earlier commentators most likely had in mind Mount Hermon not far to the north.

It was for Merrill a fact beyond doubt that Caesarea Philippi was the place where Jesus asked his disciples: "Who do people say that the Son of Man is?" Yet he did not refer explicitly to the "bold cliff of limestone" as his account of Caesarea Philippi came to a dramatic climax: Caesarea Philippi, he wrote, "had natural beauty and wealth; it had costly public buildings, temples, and marble gods. Emotions of a peculiar character are wakened in the mind when we consider the fact that Jesus of Nazareth looked upon all these things. On the one hand were the military power of Rome and pagan idolatry in its most fascinating forms, and on the other Christ and his disciples, a humble band; but the Master utters to one of them the notable words: 'Thou art Peter, and upon this Rock I will build my church; and the gates of hell shall not prevail against it'."[31]

The rest was rather anticlimactic: "This city, famous for the visits and works of kings, emperors, and victorious generals, was honoured also by the presence of Christ. This is, however, but one of the many strange contrasts which meet us at almost every turn as we study the history of this land."[32]

For all his failure to do theological justice to that "bold cliff of limestone" Merrill clearly said enough, to say nothing of the two magnificent illustrations, to enable the many theologians who read his work to turn that "bold cliff" into a backdrop for the words by which Jesus declared Simon to be the Rock. Instead, a deliberate effort was made almost immediately by two German scholars, Georg Ebers and Hermann Guthe, to foreclose the possibility of recognizing in that cliff such a natural backdrop. They did so as they hastened to bring out Wilson's work, with all its illustrations, in a free German translation.[33]

Actually, Ebers and Guthe took rude liberties with the English original as they were rendering Merrill's reflections on Christ and Caesarea Philippi. According to Ebers and Guthe: "Caesarea Philippi has a special significance for us through the fact that it was visited by Jesus. As Jesus travelled from Bethsaida up to the headwaters of the Jordan, he asked his disciples about the opinion of the people concerning his own person and finally about the opinion of his disciples. It was on that journey that Peter answered him: 'You are Christ, the Son of the living God' (Mk 8:27 ff; Mt 16:13 ff). It was in that area that Christ let his disciples have their first glimpse into the sad future of suffering and death in store for him (Mk 8:31). It then became clear how very human were still the thoughts of Peter who had just made his confession of faith in the Messiah. He saw in Jesus the Savior of Israel, who would restore the unforgettable kingdom of David. Would now this Jesus be rejected and killed by the elders, high priests, and scribes? Peter bade Jesus to preserve his life, to diminish the danger. But Jesus replied in a tone of deep unwillingness to this temptation coming to him from the very leader of his followers: 'Get out of my sight, you Satan! You are not judging by God's standards but by man's!' These serious and most meaningful conversations of Jesus with his disciples have made hallowed the area of Caesarea Philippi and according to the account of the Gospels, which made the report about the transfiguration of Jesus immediately follow these conversations, we must conclude that this event [the transfiguration] also had taken place in the neighborhood of Caesarea Philippi on a high mountain."[34]

In departing from Merrill's text, which in most other cases they followed closely, Ebers and Guthe obeyed a pattern. It had been set by a long-standing Protestant tradition aimed at slighting the significance of Peter as the Rock. That pattern equally determined the use which, a dozen or so years after the publication of Wilson's work, was made of it in that connection in a book which itself was to set a pattern. The book in question was *The Historical Geography of the Holy Land Especially in Relation to the History of Israel and of the Early Church* by George Adam Smith. The work had set that pattern by going through more than 25 editions in less than 40 years following its first publication in 1894.[35]

Since Smith's book was meant to be a manual to be used by students of theology, Smith, who heavily relied on Wilson's work, did his best to correlate Bible and landscape. Thus Smith quoted with relish some psalms relating to the cascades of the Jordan's headwaters. He was delighted in seeing in the rocky wall, in the cult of Pan at its bottom, in the temple of Augustus on its top, in the coins attesting the long presence of Pan's priests there, so many proofs that this was the scene where Christ's divine origin was fittingly recognized for the first time. But Smith did not recall that the recognition was made by Peter, nor did he say anything about Jesus' words to Peter declaring him the Rock on which he was to build his church, against which the jaws of death would never prevail.

Such omission could hardly be unintentional. A Protestant's uneasiness (although Merrill's clear reference to Peter the Rock is a perfect counterexample) about those words must have been at work when Smith emphasized that Christ insisted there on his being the Son of God as opposed to earthly rulers calling themselves such; on his eternal though otherworldly reign as opposed to the worldly but transitory rule of Caesar; on his impending crucifixion as opposed to a pagan enjoyment of life; and on the need that his disciples submit to one another rather than trying, like pagans, to lord it over one another.

The points emphasized by Smith were perfectly valid. But none of them was the most valid point in that geographic context which was his professed aim to emphasize. That most valid point was the correlation between the wall of rock at Banias and the words Christ spoke there to Peter. For more than twenty years countless readers, including many professional theologians and biblical scholars, failed to notice this, thus revealing some of the binding force that dogmatic presuppositions can have on the thinking of any theologian.

Something of that binding force was still subtly present when Otto Immisch, a Lutheran pastor and theologian in Freiburg, Germany, first spelled out in 1916 in an unambiguous manner the correlation in question. He insisted that the correlation must not be given relevance for Church history (one would rather say ecclesiology today), while he acknowledged that the most specific point in Matthew's account implied a reference to that wall of rock as the actual background for Christ's declaring Simon to be the Rock. By not recognizing this point, Immisch declared, Smith failed to make the "decisive step."[36]

The article by Immisch who modestly called his paper a set of "lay remarks," was a reply to an effort which aimed to show that the words uttered at Caesarea Philippi were Matthew's invention.[37] Immisch argued against this claim also with a summary of the archaeological research done at Banias since Smith's and Guerin's books were published.[38] An interesting result of those explorations was a likely identification of the site of Augustus' temple. A 200-year-old mosque on the site and the huge cave form the focal points of a photo published by Guthe in 1908,[39] a photo not mentioned by Immisch.[40]

That the article of Immisch created no echo in Protestant circles is understandable. It is more difficult to explain that

The wall of rock, photographed shortly before 1908
(from *Palestine*, p. 113)

Catholic biblical scholars found no food for thought in it. It was for all practical purposes dismissed in 1923 in the famous commentary on the Gospel of Matthew by J. M. Lagrange, who wrote: "It would be too much in the way of precision to imagine the scene [of Christ's words to Peter] at the source of the Jordan. Immisch has thought that Jesus' answer to Peter had been inspired by the stage: a grotto which evoked the opening of the hell, the temple of Augustus built on the rock. This is ingenious but without support in the text.[41]

For Lagrange the absence of support was the fact that Luke (9:18-22) did not tie Peter's confession of faith to a specific place, and according to Matthew (16:13) it took place merely "in the neighborhood of Caesarea Philippi." Worse, according to Mark (8:27) it took place "on the way" to the villages around Caesarea Philippi. Clearly, Lagrange's handling of this was an all-or-nothing approach. He should have remembered that such an approach best suited the rationalist critics who were the chief targets of his still classic commentaries on the gospels.

Lagrange notwithstanding, Mark and especially Matthew brought Peter's confession of faith close enough to Caesarea Philippi. If Immisch's argument was indeed "ingenious," then it would have been genuinely in keeping with the methodology of a Catholic biblical scholar of Lagrange's stature and commitment to weigh carefully the possibilities of that argument. It seems indeed that Lagrange's enormous impact on Catholic biblical scholars did nip in the bud any willingness on their part to look up Immisch's article and make their own judgment on its merits.

Curiously, not even the sight of that wall of rock has caused second thoughts among those Catholic biblical scholars who, since World War I, and especially since World War II, have studied and worked in the Holy Land.[42] Of course, not all of them travelled as far as Banias. Only for the past twenty years has it been possible for an ordinary tourist to travel from Tel Aviv or Jerusalem to northern Galilee on a regularly scheduled basis. Banias has become part of tours only since 1967. Even today most pilgrims to the Holy Land hardly ever venture farther to the north than Nazareth and the Sea of Galilee.

But the really telling point, and here Immisch's article is of no help, is not the geological and archaeological background of Jesus' words to Peter, but their biblical background. To work out that background would have been the obvious task of biblical scholars, often notorious for their eagerness to clear up every small detail in semantics and lexicology. Although they did not leave wholly untouched the usage of the word "rock" in the Old Testament, they hardly paid attention commensurate to the fact, easily ascertainable from any better concordance, that in the Old Testament only God is called rock. Before the present ecumenical open-mindedness made itself felt, Protestant scholars had shown no real interest in the topic, a fact understandable only to a certain extent. For even if Peter's faith is taken for the rock, this still leaves one with much to consider about the fact that apart from that faith of Peter only God is called rock in the written word of God. Raised on such magnificent hymns as the "Rock of Ages," Protestants might have been expected to resonate on hearing the words of Christ to Peter, but they did not, partly because they rarely heard those very words preached and partly because they were prone to take them for the Trojan horse of Roman Catholicism. Since the recent rise of ecumenical spirit and mutual respect, the construction of theological Trojan horses has, of course, lost that veneer of respectability which it might have had only twenty years ago.

This is not to suggest that the Old Testament usage of the word "rock" failed to be recalled for such tactics in Oscar Cullmann's famous book, *Peter: Disciple, Apostle, and Martyr*, first published in 1952.[43] The book is a classic in cutting both ways and also in undercutting itself. On the one hand, it dealt the *coup de grâce* to the traditional Protestant interpretation that Christ meant Peter's faith and not Peter himself in speaking of him as a rock. On the other hand, it presented Peter as a *primus inter pares,* or one of the triumvirate of which James and John were the other members, a conclusion clearly destructive of the Roman Catholic position. But by erecting a chasm between the apostolic and the postapostolic Church,[44] it undercut the consistency of the ties of all Christians, Catholic and Protestant, with the Church founded by Christ on the apostles. Among those ties is the New Testament itself as document whose authoritative, divinely inspired character can be assured only by a Church teaching in the name of Christ.

Had Cullmann paid close attention to the Old Testament usage of the word "rock," he might have sensed the incongruity of lowering Peter, the Rock, to the rank of others whom Christ did not call rock. Cullmann's oversight may easily appear justified if one pages through Charles (later Cardinal) Journet's *The Primacy of Peter.*[45] In this classic pre-Vatican II Roman Catholic reply to Cullmann, he offers no hint about the biblical background of Simon being named and constituted a Rock, a background far more telling than that huge wall of rock in the neighborhood of Caesarea Philippi. Ten years later, in 1963, that biblical background was equally overlooked in Otto Karrer's *Peter and the Church,*[46] which emphasizes the inconsistencies and pitfalls of Cullmann's thesis rather than Roman Catholic dogma. Another ten years later the background in question was not found worthy of mention by the distinguished Roman Catholic participant in a Protestant-Catholic symposium published under the title, *Peter in the New Testament,*[47] although the Old Testament was not at all ignored in it.

Concerning Catholic theologians, most of them priests, it should also be noted that from the late 1940's they have had the advantage of reciting a Latin psalter translated from the Hebrew and free of some obscurities of the Vulgate. Of course, the Vulgate was not responsible for the decision of the pious translators of the Hebrew Bible into the Greek Septuagint to render references to "God my Rock" as "God my Strength" and the like. Unlike the Vulgate, the new Latin translation of the

Psalms contained a dozen or so passages in which God was referred to as *petra mea,* "my rock."

Catholic theologians and priests exposed week after week to such passages might have readily made the association between God-petra and Simon-Petrus and through it might have felt a prompting to explore its biblical ramifications. Neither did they, nor the innumerable others who from the late 1950's were treated to such an excellent translation into the vernacular as the Jerusalem Bible and the many translations it inspired. Strangely enough, even in the highly acclaimed *Dictionary of the Bible* by John L. McKenzie it is only in the article "Peter" that a brief hint of the association between God-petra and Simon-Petrus is made but none in the article "Rock."[48]

Possibly, McKenzie did not elaborate on this point lest his scholarship be suspected of denominational apologetics in an ecumenical age. Yet, ecumenism implies the willingness to be informed ecumenically, that is, informed about all aspects and any and all questions that separate *and* unite Christians. Among the questions that separate them, none is in a sense more crucial than the Peter-question. Thanks largely to Cullmann, the question is no longer confused by the claim born in the heat of controversies that Christ's words to Simon referred to his faith. The Peter-question has now re-entered its logical place, which is the question about the nature and structure of the Church as predicated on its connection with Christ.

This question is not considered in this essay. Written by a Roman Catholic, this essay is offered to Protestants and Catholics alike, though more to Catholics. The only constructive reform is self-reform, a principle valid for individual Christians as well as for particular Churches. A Catholic desirous of reform should work above all on reforming himself and his views and thus help fellow Catholics do the same.

As for Protestants this essay is offered as a modest means to broaden their perspective of the Peter-question partly through its Old Testament background and partly through the spiritual drama which it implied for Peter himself. It is hoped that the same effect will be achieved in the Catholic readers within a particular perspective.

The perspective in question is determined by the impact of a small but vociferous group of Catholics who seem to think that by setting themselves up in opposition to the pope they serve the cause of ecumenism. Opposition to popes can, of course, have more than one valid form. Resistance to political and economic misuses of papal power is a case in point. Even with respect to a wide area of ecclesiastical discipline and customs, an indiscriminate use of papal power has invariably prompted rightful resistance to it.

But a Catholic makes no ecumenical contribution when he engages in homiletical, catechetical, journalistic, and literary filibusters against the pope, after the pope has spoken clearly and repeatedly on grave matters, both spiritual and disciplinary. Such a tactic goes counter to that very pastoral rule which is at the heart of the ecumenism proclaimed by Vatican II. If, according to that rule, one should help prevent the further fragmenting of any Christian communion, the Roman Catholic communion should also be protected from the threat of disunity. Such a pastoral rule will appear self-defeating only to those who seek their own ecumenical triumph while charging their own communion and, above all, its shepherd, with triumphalism.

The extent to which such spiritual self-seeking can prove destructive was well illustrated by the cover story of the November 22, 1968, issue of *Time* magazine.[49] Only three short years after the completion of Vatican II, enough material had already accrued (with due consideration for most weeklies' bent for exaggeration and sensationalism) to justify a cover story. The essence of the story was grippingly told on the cover itself, which showed, above the pope's saddened face, the keys of Peter breaking into pieces—a powerful evocation of the allegedly widespread disregard among Catholics for papal authority. Undoubtedly, a considerable number of Catholics—priests and laity—reached the conclusion that Vatican II had set them at liberty to take the keys of the Kingdom entrusted to Peter and his successors into their own hands. This process was in part supported by a superficial reading of the documents of Vatican II and by a veneer of theological scholarship infecting much that was published in the immediate wake of Vatican II.

A good example of the veneer was that, more than a decade after the publication of Cullmann's *Peter*, some younger Catholic priests claimed that Christ's words to Peter referred not to Peter but to his faith. In those years some Americans reacted to Pope John XXIII's encyclical *Mater et Magistra*[50] with the slogan "Mater si, Magistra no," giving an indication of attitudes that were developing toward the teaching authority of the Church. The slogan bespoke the inability of some conservatives to see that the Church is more than an issue of particular customs and social conditions.

Almost ten years later *Time* was able to prove with no difficulty (again in a splashy cover story, May 24, 1976),[51] that U.S. Catholicism was a Church divided. The division was illustrated by a cross made up of two separate sides. The right side was of wood, of old-fashioned shape, and hung from an outmoded golden necklace. On the left side, with straight modern edges, were painted the Stars and Stripes. The message was unequivocal: Catholicism was acceptable to some Catholics only if it strictly conformed to the norms of their particular place and time.

As to the documents of Vatican II, one of them, which will undoubtedly give much food for thought to future Church historians, was hardly read, if comments and references are an indication of what is actually being read. The document, a brief appendix to the document known as the Dogmatic Constitution on the Church, is noteworthy not only for its contents but also for its form. It contains not the deliberations of the Bishops gathered in the Council and not even their declarations, but an interpretation of what is known as their collegiality. That interpretation was not drawn up by them but was communicated to them "from higher authority." The "higher authority" was the Bishop of Rome, the only authority which, according to Roman Catholic teaching, surpasses that of any and all the bishops.

According to that communication[52] the College of Bishops, which includes the Bishop of Rome, is not to be understood as a group of equals "who entrust their power to their president." Three other points in that communication further emphasized that the notion of the collegiality of the bishops is not to be taken for a ground of rivalry between the College of Bishops and the Pope, the head of that College. In those three points emphasis is laid on the hierarchical communion with that head of the Church as condition of membership in that College; on the organic inclusion of the notion of the head in the concept of a collegiate body; and finally on the discontinuous nature of the exercise of that full power which belongs to that College. The communication declared that the head "preserves intact in the College his role of Vicar of Christ and shepherd of the universal Church." Thus while the College exercises its full power only "with the consent of its head," the head or Sovereign Pontiff, "can always exercise his authority as he chooses, as is demanded by his office itself."

The points emphasized in that communication should be of no special interest to anyone familiar and content with Roman Catholic dogma, whether he is a layman, a theologian, or a future Church historian. What will be of interest to the latter is the insertion of that communication into the documents of Vatican II and on command "from higher authority." The insertion reflected a sense of urgency or at least of caution. As subsequent events showed, both urgency and caution were appropriate.

Students of general or ecumenical councils know all too well that almost all such gatherings, especially those restricted to Latin Christendom from the Middle Ages on, witnessed the presence of forces that tried, in various degrees, to set the council over the pope. Such forces asserting themselves during Vatican II came as a great surprise to many a theologian and to a great majority of clergy and laity. The surprise was both unjustified and justified. There was little justification for the simplicity, if not naiveté, which took for granted that the strict centralization, by which the papacy exercised its power for the previous one hundred years or so, would last forever. Whatever the endurance of the papacy, its style of action has always been a product of the times. And the times were rapidly changing in the wake of World War II. The changes unhinged peoples and customs with a violence which history rarely witnessed before. Only naiveté could hope for unchanging style in the papacy while all other styles were changing at an accelerated rate.

Certainly justified in that great surprise was the finding that some Catholics took the change of style as an opportunity for changing the substance concerning the position of hierarchy in the church and the position of the pope in the hierarchy. Of these two targets, the one relating to the position of the pope within the hierarchy drew by far the greater attention. The change relating to the position of the hierarchy was also part of a logic which is never satisfied with half measures. Catholics, thinking that the College of Bishops, or the bishops of a particular national conference, or the local bishop had now been enthroned above the pope, soon demanded the same throne for themselves when the new "supreme authorities" did not yield to their whims and fancies in matters of faith, morals, and discipline.

Seeing this clamor for substantial change, Catholics who still believed in the supreme position of the pope could only be surprised if not deeply upset. Some of them, especially converts, thought that the Church had in fact gone mad.[53] It could be of little comfort for them to muse that were a Pius X, a Pius XI or a Pius XII still alive, no plea for disloyalty would be tolerated for however brief a time.

But now papal tolerance seemed to have no bounds. What is worse, the evangelical patience of two popes, John XXIII and Paul VI, was taken all too often for a weakness which had no choice but to tolerate even rank disloyalty. Actually, those two popes, and especially Paul, on whose shoulders fell the burden of steering the ship of the Church along currents charted by the documents of Vatican II, displayed an unusual measure of endurance.

Their patient endurance displayed something of their sharing that function of that rock which is Peter. That function reserved for a human called and declared to be rock will appear truly biblical and therefore superhuman only by recalling that before Simon was called and constituted rock by the Son of God, only God was called Rock in the written word of God.

God is called Rock in the Bible because he is absolutely superior to the vicissitudes of history and is therefore the only safeguard against them. As to the papacy, it strikes the outside observer mainly by its endurance. Very modern insiders, who pen books with such titles as *The Final Conclave*[54] and *Le dernier pape,*[55] only prove by their shortsightedness the truth of the long view taken in a famous passage which Macaulay, an outsider, wrote over a hundred years ago. The passage is part of Macaulay's review of Ranke's *History of the Popes,* a book in which the papacy was not given much lease on life.[56] Were Macaulay to write today, with the British Empire completely gone, he would not conjure up—to illustrate the contrast between the transitoriness of empires and the endurance of the papacy—a traveler from New Zealand sketching the ruins of St. Paul's from a decayed London Bridge.[57] Perhaps today he would portray his imaginary tourist drawing the scattered pieces of Lenin's tomb, or of Washington's obelisk, or of Peking's Heavenly Gate, to evoke the very distant future which would still not be without a pope in the chair of Peter.[58]

But the more that endurance reveals of itself, the more it becomes clear that its core is not the endurance of power but

the patience to endure any power, be it the power of willful in-
dividuals, lay or ecclesiastic, and of political and cultural pressure groups. That is the kind of patience which was enjoined on
all Christians, tempted time and again with the triumphalist
urge to clear the wheatfield of all cockles sown by the enemy.
Such humbling patience is the only effective antidote to triumphalism, a patience which is never a condoning of the evil
but an endurance of it. Such a patience, which must have the
quality of a rock that outlasts all storms lashing at it, shall only
come from the kind of experience which made Paul exclaim:
"When I am powerless, it is then that I am strong."[59]

Sensing his own weakness made Paul humbly reach out for
the strength of God, the Rock. Therefore the core of the mys-
tery of a mere man being called and made rock by the Son of
God, ought to be a most humbling experience. It consists in the
endurance of true humility, a point vividly illustrated by the
spiritual odyssey of Simon, son of Jonah.

Once viewed in that perspective, the words spoken by
Christ to Simon will not become so many occasions for dissent
but a humble and humbling call for union, which can come only
in the measure in which true humility grows in the hearts of all
Christians. Humility in turn will provide readiness to face up to
the full biblical background of Christ's words to Peter at Caesarea Philippi.

The neglect of a conspicuous wall of rock there is a reminder of that oversight which was the most conspicuous attitude toward the Word while dwelling patiently among us. He
experienced the burden of that patience to the point of ex-
claiming, "how long shall I be with you!" (Luke 14:22), and
warned us that patience alone can safeguard one's soul in the
midst of trials, the ever-present condition of the Church and of
all Christians who do not wish to be greater than their Master.

NOTES

[1]*The Jewish War,* I, 21, 3. See *Josephus* with English translation in nine volumes (Loeb Classical Library; Cambridge, Mass.: Harvard University Press, 1926-65), vol II, p. 191. Josephus also notes that the temple Herod erected at Panias was only one of the many pagan temples he built throughout the Holy Land.

[2]The pool was called *phiale* or saucer for its circular shape, and therefore Josephus most likely had in mind the circular lake Birket Ram five miles east of Banias. The underground passage of water from this lake to Banias remains unproven.

[3]*The Jewish War,* III, 10, 7; in *Josephus,* vol. II, pp. 719-21.

[4]*Jewish Antiquities,* XV, 10, 3; in *Josephus,* vol. VIII, pp. 175-76.

[5]Ibid., XX, 9, 4; in *Josephus,* vol. IX, p. 501. Long before Josephus, Panias was mentioned twice by the great Greek historian, Polybius (203? B.C.-c. 120 B.C.), as the scene of the great battle (169 B.C.) between Antiochus of Syria and Scopas, a general of Ptolemy, ruler of Egypt. See *Polybius: The Histories,* with an English translation by W. R. Paton (Loeb Classical Library; London: William Heinemann, 1927) vol. V, p. 37 and vol. VI, p. 3.

[6]There had been a dozen or so English, French, and German translations already in the two centuries preceding William Whiston's memorable translation published in 1737, which in turn started another wave of translations.

[7]Of the two passages *(Jewish Antiquities,* XVIII, 3, 3 and XX, 9, 1; see *Josephus,* vol. IX, pp. 49-51 and 497), the former, a rather favorable presentation of Jesus, had long been suspected to be in part a reworking by a Christian copyist. That the original form of that passage may have been preserved in a Syriac manuscript of the 10th century was contended in the early 1970's by two scholars at Hebrew University. Neither of them suggested the conclusion drawn by *Time* (Feb. 28, 1972, p. 55) that their work "weakens the credibility of the text—even as a proof of Jesus' existence," a conclusion typical of propagandistic journalism.

[8]*Travels in Syria and the Holy Land by the Late Jean Louis Burckhardt.* Published by the Association for Promoting the Discovery of the Interior Parts of Africa (London: J. Murray, 1822). On Burckhardt, see K. Sim, *Desert Traveller: The Life of John Lewis Burckhardt* (London: Gollancz, 1969).

[9]*Johann Ludwig Burckhardt's Reisen in Syria, Palestina und der*

Gegend des Berges Sinai, edited from the English and provided with annotations by W. Gesenius (Weimar: Verlag des Gr. S. priv. Landes-Industrie-Comptoirs, 1823) in 2 vols.

[10]*Travels in Syria,* p. 40.

[11]Burckhardt's phrase, "the largest niche is above a spacious cavern, under which the river rises," is at best misleading even if the "cavern" (p. 38) is taken not for the sanctuary but for the cave.

[12]These pools are of recent construction.

[13]*Description géographique, historique et archéologique de la Palestine,* of which the third part dealing with Galilee in two volumes was printed in 1880 (Paris: Imprimerie Nationale). Its entire chapter 99 is devoted to Banias (vol. II, pp. 308-23). Guerin (1821-91) was a member of the Ecole d'Athènes since 1852 and during his last forty years he traveled eight times in the Near Orient.

[14]There is no inscription in honor "of the God Pan, son of Jupiter, lover of Eros," as claimed by D. Ridolfi, *Simon Pierre, rocher biblique* (Paris: Apostolat des Editions, 1965), p. 98, a work which became available to me only when the text of this book was being prepared for typesetting. See also note 35 of Chapter II.

[15]*Numismatique de la Terre Sainte: Description des monnais autonomes et impériales de la Palestine et de l'Arabie Petrée* (Paris: J. Rotschild, 1874). Louis-Félicien-Joseph Caignart de Saulcy (1807-1880) was an enormously productive archaeologist and after 1842 a member of the Académie des Inscriptions et Belles-Lettres.

[16]In classical mythology Syrinx was "a mountain nymph of Arcadia who was transformed, in order to protect her chastity from Pan, into the reed from which Pan then made the panpipe." See *The Random House Dictionary of the English Language* (1966), p. 1443.

[17]See L. R. Farnell, *The Cults of the Greek States,* vol. V (Oxford: Clarendon Press, 1909), p. 431.

[18]Ibid, p. 434. The prayer is from *Phaedrus,* 279B.

[19]*Numismatique de la Terre Sainte,* p. 317.

[20]Published in London (Virtue & Co., 1880-84) in four quarto volumes. An American edition was published in New York (D. Appleton, 1881-84) in two quarto volumes. References will be to the American edition.

[21]For a short account of Wilson's life, see "Wilson, Sir Charles William," in *Dictionary of National Biography.* Second Supplement, vol. 3 (London: Smith, Elder & Co., 1912), pp. 687-89.

[22]*Picturesque Palestine,* vol. I, pp. 335-59.

[23]Sir Charles William Wilson, *The Land of Galilee & the North,* with an introduction by Z. Vilnay (Jerusalem: Ariel Publishing House,

1975).

[24]*Picturesque Palestine*, vol. I, p. 352.

[25]Ibid. Variations in estimating the height of that wall of rock are due to the possibility of making several choices for its true baseline.

[26]Ibid., p. 356. As to Josephus, see his *The Jewish War*, III, 9, 7; in *Josephus*, vol. II, p. 701.

[27]Ibid., and *The Jewish War*, VII, 2, 1; in *Josephus*, vol. III, pp. 511-13.

[28]Ibid.

[29]See *A Select Library of Nicene and post-Nicene Fathers*, Volume I, *Eusebius* (Grand Rapids, Mich: Wm. B. Eerdmans, 1952), p. 304.

[30]*Picturesque Palestine*, vol. I, p. 356.

[31]Ibid., pp. 356-57.

[32]Ibid., p. 357.

[33]*Palestina in Bild und Wort. Nebst der Sinaihalbinsel und dem Lande Gosen* (Stuttgart and Leipzig: Deutsche Verlags-Anstalt, 1883-84). Ebers was an Egyptologist, Guthe was professor of theology at the University of Leipzig and editor (1878-96) of the Journal of the German Palestine Society.

[34]Ibid., vol. I, p. 364.

[35]Originally published in Great Britain in 1894. The American edition (New York: A.C. Armstrong and Son, 1895) already carried the label "fourth thousand." Its section on Banias (pp. 473-79) remained unchanged even in the 25th ("revised throughout") edition (London: Hodder and Stoughton, 1931). This complete silence on Peter the Rock is perpetuated in M. F. Unger, *Archaeology and the New Testament* (Grand Rapids, Mich.: Zondervan, 1962), pp. 132-36.

[36]O. Immisch, "Mattheus 16, 18. Laienbemerkungen zu der Untersuchung Dells," *Zeitschrift für neutestamentliche Wissenschaft* 17 (1916), pp. 18-26. For quotation, see p. 19.

[37]The effort was the article by A. Dell, "Mattheus 16, 17-19," ibid., 15 (1914), pp. 1-49.

[38]Art. cit., p. 20. The list of works cited by Immisch contained the German translation by Ebers and Guthe of Wilson's *Picturesque Palestine,* but not the English original. If Immisch had had access to the original, he would have most likely noticed not only the liberties taken by the German translators but also that Merrill had almost made "the decisive step."

[39]Since Guthe's *Palestina* (Bielefield and Leipzig: Verhagen und Klasing, 1908) was a volume (XXI) in the very popular series, *Land und Leute*, the photo in question (p. 113) must have come to the attention of many theologians both in Germany and abroad.

[40]My perusal of other, also German, works cited by Immisch suggests that their authors were not familiar with the English text of Merrill.

[41]*Evangile selon Saint Matthieu* (Paris: J. Gabalda, 1923). In the 8th edition (1948) the passage quoted (p. 322) was identical with that in the first.

[42]A good measure of that insensitivity is the article "Caesarea Philippi" by P. Horvath in the *New Catholic Encyclopedia* (New York: McGraw-Hill, 1967), vol. II, p. 1046.

[43]The English translation by F. V. Filson was published the following year (Philadelphia: Westminster Press). The English translation of the second revised and expanded edition (same translator and publisher) appeared in 1962. Cullmann's reference to *Golgotha* (Leipzig: E. Pfeiffer, 1926) by J. Jeremias, in a sense also a study of the significance of the idea of rock in the Old and New Testaments, is revealing. Cullmann failed to see that Jeremias overlooked a large number of scriptural passages, and especially those which relate to God as the Rock. As to Cullmann's endorsement (pp. 186 in the English translation of the first edition, and p. 193 in the English translation of the second edition) of the reference in Isaiah to Abraham as rock (a reference also endorsed in *Golgotha*, p. 74), see notes 10 and 11 of Chapter III.

[44]The ultimate source of that chasm is Cullmann's notion of "biblical" time, a notion originating not so much in the Bible as in the nominalist philosophical and theological tradition initiated by Ockham. That tradition had been anticipated (under the impact of a Koran lacking the balance secured by the notion of the always consistent God of the Bible) in the position represented by the great Muslim theologians, al-Ashari and al-Ghazzali, a position which among other things undermined the prospects of a vigorous scientific enterprise among the Arabs of old. (For details, see my Gifford Lectures, *The Road of Science and the Ways to God* [Chicago: University of Chicago Press; Edinburgh: Scottish Academic Press, 1978] pp. 40-43 and 411-13, and my *Science and Creation: From Eternal Cycles to an Oscillating Universe* [Edinburgh: Scottish Academic Press; New York: Science History Publications, 1974], pp. 204-05.) In Cullmann's case a most revealing consequence of that allegedly biblical notion of time is the error which he attributes to Jesus concerning the time of his second coming! See pp. 201 and 207 in the English translation of the first and second editions, respectively.

[45]Translated from the French (1953) by J. Chapin (Westminster, Md.: Newmann Press).

[46]Translated from the German (1963) by R. Walls (Montreal: Palm Publishers).

[47]*Peter in the New Testament,* edited by R. E. Brown, and others (Minneapolis: Augsburg Publishing House, 1973). For a similar omission by Brown, see his *The Gospel according to John I-XII* with introduction, translation and notes (Garden City, N.Y.: Doubleday, 1966), especially p. 80.

[48]New York: Macmillan, 1973, p. 665.

[49]"Catholic Freedom v. Authority," pp. 42-49. According to the condescending advice given by *Time* to the pope, "some Catholic voices calling for reform he may rightfully ignore as imprudent or irresponsible" (p. 49), but Catholic readers of issues of the last 10 years of *Time* are still to be treated to an unequivocal paragraph, let alone to a cover story, on those "irresponsible" voices.

[50]Any study of it, however brief, would easily show that John XXIII, for many the paradigm of a "pastoral" pope, that is, a pope abdicating his authority, did not part with the tradition of the previous encyclicals teaching with authority. It was, in fact, by relying on his authority that he convoked Vatican II, and secured thereby its basis of authority.

[51]"A Church Divided," pp. 48-59. The illustration of the cover was possibly inspired by the jacket of *Nationalism and American Catholicism* by D. Dohen (New York: Sheed and Ward, 1967).

[52]For its English translation, W. M. Abbott (ed.) *The Documents of Vatican II* (New York: Guild Press, 1966), p. 97-101.

[53]A consideration which motivated John Eppstein's book, *Has the Catholic Church Gone Mad?* (London: Tom Stacey, 1971). The American edition (New Rochelle, N. Y.; Arlington House) was already in its third printing by August, 1972.

[54]New York: Stein & Day, 1978. Its author M. Martin, once a confidant of the late Cardinal Bea, cannot, of course, be held entirely responsible for the declaration on the flyleaf of the jacket: "When Luther pinned his message to the door, the result was an unstoppable revolution. With this book, Dr. Martin, a former Jesuit whose laicization was granted by Pope Paul, may be said to have pinned his message to the door of St. Peter's. As always, there will be some who will call *The Final Conclave* an act of treason; if so, the Declaration of Independence was an act of treason. This is a book in a grand tradition, a speculation that fairly, realistically, and movingly introduces us to the possibility of a future most of humanity would hope to avoid."

[55]Paris: Editions Pygmalion, 1977. Its author, Jean-Anne Chatelet, published a year earlier *Monseigneur Lefèvre.*

[56]The German original of Ranke's *Ecclesiastical and Political History of the Popes during the Sixteenth and Seventeenth Centuries* was first published in 1834-36. The papacy survived even the onslaught of the Reformation only because, in Ranke's view, some races cannot find an intellectual and emotional resting place between the extremes of unbelief and superstition, a point endorsed in a way of conclusion in Macaulay's review of Ranke's work.

[57]The passage forming the introductory part of what is possibly the best among Macaulay's famous essays deserves to be quoted in full partly because of its literary merit and partly because of younger Catholics' unfamiliarity with it:

"There is not, and there never was, on this earth, a work of human policy so well deserving of examination as the Roman Catholic Church. The history of that Church joins together the two great ages of human civilization. No other institution is left standing which carries the mind back to the times when the smoke of sacrifice rose from the Pantheon, and when camelopards and tigers bounded in the Flavian amphitheatre. The proudest royal houses are but of yesterday, when compared with the line of the Supreme Pontiffs. That line we trace back to an unbroken series, from the pope who crowned Napoleon in the nineteenth century, to the Pope who crowned Pepin in the eighth; and far beyond the time of Pepin the august dynasty extends, till it is lost in the twilight of fable. The republic of Venice came next in antiquity. But the republic of Venice was modern when compared with the Papacy; and the republic of Venice is gone, and the Papacy remains. The Papacy remains, not in decay, not a mere antique; but full of life and youthful vigour. The Catholic Church is still sending forth to the farthest ends of the world, missionaries as zealous as those who landed in Kent with Augustin; and still confronting hostile kings with the same spirit with which she confronted Attila. The number of her children is greater than in any former age. Her acquisitions in the New World have more than compensated her for what she has lost in the Old. Her spiritual ascendency extends over the vast countries which lie between the plains of the Missouri and Cape Horn—countries which, a century hence, may not improbably contain a population as large as that which now inhabits Europe. The members of her communion are certainly not fewer than a hundred and fifty million; and it will be difficult to show that all the other Christian sects united, amount to a hundred and twenty millions. Nor do we see any sign which indicates the term of her long domination is approaching. She saw the commencement of all governments, and of all the ecclesiastical establishments, that now exist in the world; and we feel no assurance that she is not destined to see the end of them all. She was great and respected before the Saxon had set foot on Britain—before the Frank had passed the Rhine—when Grecian eloquence still flourished at Antioch—when idols were still worshipped in the temple of Mecca. And she may still exist in undiminished vigour when some traveller from New Zealand shall, in the midst of a vast solitude, take his stand on a broken arch of London Bridge to sketch the ruins of St. Paul's"—*Edinburgh Review* 72 (1840), pp. 227-28.

[58]Or perhaps a latter-day Macaulay would recall Anatole France's vision of a future pope, who earns his living as an obscure shoemaker in a dark alley in Rome, and comment on it with the words which Mark Twain wired from London to the editor of that American newspaper which had just reported his death: "Your news about my having passed away is somewhat premature."

[59]2 Cor 12:10.

II. God the Rock

In the Old Testament God is first addressed as Rock (*sur*) in the great farewell of Moses,[1] the mediator of the covenant between Yahweh and his people. A farewell is always a poignant affair, and this one was particularly so for Moses and the Israelites. After forty years of wandering through the rock-strewn wilderness of Sinai, the moment of truth came both for Moses and for the people. Only once did Moses yield to doubts about the promises of Yahweh, but this was enough to deprive him of the right to enter the land of promise. Such was God's judgment on the one who was given power to split the sea to produce dry passage through the waters, and to split the rock to make water flow in the desert.

Moses was to die when the hour came to make the long-sought, long-postponed step into the promised land. Shortly beforehand, Moses once more read the terms of the Covenant, or the Law, which was placed in the ark, ready to be carried across the Jordan, a more fateful crossing for the people than the crossing of the Red Sea with Pharaoh in pursuit. On the other side of the Red Sea no enemy lay in wait. On the other side of the Jordan tribe upon tribe, city upon city, were ready to oppose the invaders. It was a foolhardy venture by human count, but a venture not based on human strategy. The Jews must have had an army, but it was to be of no avail unless they relied on Yahweh's strength.[2] The future of Israel would rest on their willingness to accept God for what he is, the only solid foundation, the only one to be called Rock.

Moses was hundred-twenty when he sang his farewell. He kept his strength to the end which could only enhance the impression made by the wisdom of old age and a long life tempered in many trials. What Moses sang about was the wisdom derived from the past for the future. If in the past the ills and woes of the people were due to their reluctance to take Yahweh for their only strength or rock, the future would implement the same pattern. The gods of the heathen were mere rocks,[3] no match for Yahweh, the Rock. This was the message to be impressed on each new generation of a people who, as Moses knew all too well, were time and again stiff-necked and unbelieving. Or as recorded in chapter 32 of Deuteronomy:

> I will sing the Lord's renown.
> Oh, proclaim the greatness of our God!
> The Rock—how faultless are his deeds,
>   how right all his ways.
> A faithful God, without deceit,
>   how just and upright he is! (Dt 32:3-4).

But for the many favors of God the Israelites took credit for themselves:

> They spurned the God who made them
>   and scorned the saving Rock (Dt 32:15).

The Israelites provoked God with their idols and merited Moses' sentence:

> You were unmindful of the Rock that begot you.
> You forgot the God who gave you birth. (Dt 32:18)

If the Israelites had sense they could remember the failure

of their enemies' gods:

> How could one man rout a thousand,
>   or two men put ten thousand to flight,
> Unless it was because their "rock" sold them
>   and the Lord delivered them up?
> Indeed, their "rock" is not like our Rock
>   and our foes are under condemnation. (Dt 32:30-31)

The Lord pledges continued protection of his people against enemies with no 'rock' to rely on:

> He will say "Where are their gods
>   whom they relied on as their 'rock'?" (Dt 32:37)

Moreover, Yahweh even raises his hand and swears that he will avenge anyone harming his servants. Moses concludes:

> Take heart, impress all these words on your
>   children (Dt 32:46).

Only the elders could hear the farewell song of Moses, but soon its words were being handed down to the rank and file.[4]

As the Israelites moved out from behind the protection of the walls of rock, they advanced toward the Jordan, seeing beyond its banks similar rocks that provided safety to anyone withdrawing to their heights.[5] The rock cliffs were a fortress. No army could overcome some of them.[6] But as Moses had told the Israelites, their final strategy was to look to Yahweh as ultimately the strongest Rock.

The strategy, although forgotten time and again, lived on and was recalled with elemental force as the Israelites became a nation. Never an easy process, the birth to nationhood was particularly difficult for the Israelites. The Canaanite tribes presented ever-new problems[7] while the strategy of Moses demanded ever-new faith in Yahweh as the only Rock. At times their faith was so weak as to let the ark fall into the hands of the Philistines.[8] It was not entirely an act of faith when the people wanted to have a king, the symbolic assurance of finally becoming a nation. That their request for a king did not turn into a self-defeating strategy was largely due to the presence of Samuel, from his birth on a symbol of the Mosaic strategy pivoted on Yahweh as its sole strength. Samuel was the child of Hannah, long-barren wife of Elkanah. On offering her son to Eli, the chief priest at Siloh, for service at the tent of Yahweh, Hannah spoke words which showed how Moses' farewell had become a part of the religious folklore. A thousand years later, Mary, the daughter of Annah, was to voice, in much the same words, her gratitude for the marvels done to her by the Lord. The strategy of Yahweh, the Rock, was valid for the people as well as for Hannah, a handmaid as low by appearance as Mary was to be:

> My heart exults in the Lord;
>   my horn is exalted in my God.
> I have swallowed up my enemies;
>   I rejoice in my victory.
> There is no Holy One like the Lord;
>   there is no Rock like our God (1 S 2:1-2).

Mary must have had these words in mind as she continued, like Hannah, to declare that the strong would be humiliated, the fat would go hungry, the hungry would be well-fed, and the poor would be seated with the rich: for the pillars of the earth are the Lord's and this is why the horn of his anointed will be exalted.

Hannah's anticipation of Mary's Magnificat was all the more proper since Hannah's son, Samuel, played a crucial role in turning the people into a nation by anointing Saul as king. Samuel's God-given authority as a judge and prophet was also the basis for transferring the office of king from Saul to David, the shepherd boy.[9] With David, the most momentous advance was made toward the specific fulfillment of the promises of the covenant. From David's loins was to be born Israel's ultimate Shepherd, leading the people to the fountain of redemption.

Like any great advance, the one tied to David's role was also an advance on rocky grounds. Saul was far from ready to yield. A life-and-death struggle ensued between the two, its tensions never fading from David's memory. On singing his final song of thanksgiving, his escape from Saul's hands became the symbol for all the cases when Yahweh had become for him the Rock of refuge:

> O Lord, my rock, my fortress, my deliverer,
>   my God, my rock of refuge!
> My shield, the horn of my salvation,
>   my stronghold, my refuge,
> My savior from violence, you keep me safe.
>   'Praised be the Lord,' I exclaim,
> and I am safe from my enemies. (2 S 22:2-4)

Since the trials of David were like so many thunderstorms and violent earthquakes, he could fittingly refer to God as the unshakable rock of safety:

> For who is God except the Lord?
>   Who is a rock except our God? . . .
> The Lord live! And blessed be my Rock!
>   Extolled be my God, Rock of salvation! (2 S 22:32, 47)

Such was the God who showed kindness to David and was to show the same kindness to his posterity forever, a prospect worthy of the finest outburst by one of history's greatest poets. That it was not a momentary outburst on his part can be grasped from the manner in which it was inscribed into the Second Book of Samuel:

> These are the last words of David:
> The utterance of David, son of Jesse;
>   the utterance of the man God raised up,

> Anointed of the God of Jacob,
> > favorite of the Mighty One of Israel.
> The Spirit of the Lord spoke through me;
> > his word was on my tongue.
> The God of Israel spoke;
> > of me the Rock of Israel said
> "He that rules over men in justice,
> > that rules in the fear of God
> Is like the morning light of sunrise
> > on a cloudless morning" (2 S 23:1-4).

In view of the absolute solidity of the promise of a God who is Rock, David could but envision the future as firmly secured:

> Is not my house firm before God?
> > He has made an eternal covenant with me,
> > set forth in detail and secured (2 S 23:5).

No wonder this great thanksgiving of David lived on also on the lips of the people in the words of Psalm 17, one of the great psalms:

> I love you, Lord, my strength,
> > my rock, my fortress, my savior.
> My God is the rock where I take refuge;
> > my shield, my mighty help, my stronghold (Ps 17:1-2).

The backdrop to God, the Rock, was the raging of a tempest, a symbol of utter insecurity and deadly threat from enemies on every side. The superior strength of Yahweh justifies the exclamation:

> For who is God but the Lord?
> Who is a rock but our God? (Ps 17:32).

A David victorious over all his enemies can but break out in praise of his God:

Long life to the Lord, my Rock! (Ps 17:47).

This was not the only psalm which one generation after
another sang of Yahweh, the Rock. The role played by the
singing in the Psalms in transforming Israel into a living
Covenant with Yahweh cannot be emphasized enough, nor can
it be described in a few words or paragraphs.[10]

Long before the Church, the New Covenant, looked upon
her official prayers molded from the Psalms as a rule of belief[11]—*lex orandi statuat legem credendi* (the norm of prayer
should set the norm of belief)—the Psalms were such a standard
in the Old Covenant. The 150 Psalms grew out of perhaps two
or three dozen composed by David, who in turn relied on an already existing tradition.[12] The depth of feeling, the soaring of
inspiration, the grip of realism and the touch of idealism—to
say nothing of the richness of poetical skill—present everywhere in the Psalms make them a unique document in the history of religious poetry. But what gives them a unique character
as a religious document, in their historical context, is the assertion that Yahweh is the only God.[13] For a people living in a land
of big and small rocks the claim took form in the image that
Yahweh is Rock, nay the sole rock, foundation, and refuge.

The Psalms were acts of popularly shared worship.
Whether the worship was public or private, the Psalms were its
backbone. Public worship was centered on the Temple in
Jerusalem and gathering around it took the form of procession.
Hardly a Jew reached the grave without having been part, on at
least a few occasions, of a procession ascending the slope of the
Temple Mount. Psalm 94, composed for such an occasion, began
with a ringing call:

Come, ring out our joy to the Lord.
Hail the rock who saves us! (Ps 94:1).

The call could not be more expressive. The Temple stood on a rock which, according to Jewish tradition, was the spot where Abraham was to have made the supreme sacrifice of his life.[14] The immolation of his only son, Isaac, was in all appearance a mockery of God's promise that in Abraham's posterity—"as countless as the stars of the sky and the sands of the seashore"—all nations of the earth would be blessed, that is, redeemed. David in turn was instructed (2 S 24:18-25) to buy the area of the rock and build an altar there so that the sacrifice offered on it would put an end to a plague decimating the Israelites. Stopping a plague was another symbol of redemption, but the symbol was strongly tied to a rock which strikes any visitor of the Mosque of Omar by its size, color, and shape.

In all evidence the rock was no longer visible once Solomon had built the Temple, but word about its striking features was passed from generation to generation. Any such rock was an invitation to some form of nature worship. Indeed, among the chief targets of the prophets' thundering were altars built on prominent rocks,[15] where Israelites could go so far in their infidelity to Yahweh as to follow the Canaanites in sacrificing children to false gods.[16]

All this must have been in the minds of those taking part in the procession advancing toward the Temple Mount. But their singing of Psalm 94 reminded them that salvation was not to be had in a physical rock, however magical in its appearance, but only in Yahweh the Rock. He was salvation in two respects. He was the foundation of the earth, representing the whole realm of physical creation. He was also the ruler of history, and especially during that phase of it, the stay in the desert, which for a Jew evoked existential uncertainty and the tragic uncertainty of man's response to God.

The same anchoring in Yahweh, the Rock, both of the universe and salvation history is embodied in Psalm 18. Its classically brief structure indicates that it must have been a most popular song. Its starting line, "the heavens declare the glory of

God," had become one of those few phrases that never wear out, though repeated as generation follows generation.[17] In that Psalm a parallel is drawn between the stability of the heavens and the enduring value of the Law. No further proof is needed to justify the conclusion:

> May the spoken words of my mouth
> the thoughts of my heart,
> win favor in your sight, O Lord,
> my rescuer, my rock! (Ps 18:15)

The theme of Yahweh, the Rock, was brought to the pious Jew in the most varied contexts. In time of danger—and were not the times such all too often?—he could pray with the words of Psalm 27:

> To you, O Lord, I call,
> my rock, hear me (Ps 27:1).

In times of happiness, he could anchor his joy in the strength of Yahweh by singing Psalm 91:

> It is good to give thanks to the Lord
> To make music in your name, O Most High
> To proclaim your love in the morning . . . .
> To proclaim that the Lord is just,
> in him, my rock, there is no wrong (Ps 91:2-3, 16).

Once he had reached old age, when he had to face the fact that "I am old and grey-headed," the pious Jew would ask Yahweh with the words of Psalm 70:

> Be a rock where I can take refuge,
> a mighty stronghold to save me;
> for you are my rock, my stronghold.
> Free me from the hand of the wicked,
> from the grip of the unjust, of the oppressor (Ps 70: 3-4).

For a Jew in exile—and how many had the experience of at least the exile of living in diaspora, that is, in pagan surroundings?—there was Psalm 41. It seems to evoke the cascades near the headwaters of the Jordan, an area where David, possibly the author of that psalm, fought pagan Canaanite tribes on at least one occasion.[18] The waters cascading down the rocky cliffs spoke of waves of instability and could remind David of the distress which ran through his own heart during his exile. In such a state it was most natural to turn to Yahweh, the Rock of stability:

> I will say to God, my rock:
> "Why have you forgotten me?
> Why do I go mourning
> Oppressed by the foe?" (Ps 41:10).

For a Jew in exile, whose heart was fainting, Psalm 60 offered a most appropriate prayer: once more because of the appropriateness of recalling Yahweh, the Rock:

> On the rock too high for me to reach
> set me on high,
> O you who have been my refuge,
> my tower against the foe (Ps 60: 3-4).

If confidence was needed, no source could be more inspiring than the words of Psalm 61 which puts emphasis on Yahweh being the sole Rock:

> In God alone is my soul at rest;
> my help comes from him.
> He alone is my rock, my stronghold,
> my fortress, I stand firm . . .
> In God alone be at rest my soul;
> for my hope comes from him
> He alone is my rock, my stronghold,
> my fortress: I stand firm.
> In God is my safety and glory,

the rock of my strength . . .
to God alone belong power and love (Ps 61:1-2, 5-6, 11-12).

Compared with God, the sole Rock, common folk could only be described in the same psalm as mere "breath" and great men were no more than "illusion," which should help one understand that no man, however great in Jewish history, was ever called rock in the Old Testament.

Yahweh, the Rock, was the supreme symbol generating confidence even when all signs of hope seemed to have vanished. Such was certainly the case of the Jew who when hanging on the cross said with the words of Psalm 30: "Into your hands I commend my spirit!" With the author of that psalm, he could have also recalled that he was the target of the crowd's slander. But there was no reason to despair as long as one was willing to say with the same Psalm:

Be a rock of refuge for me,
a mighty stronghold to save me
for you are my rock, my stronghold.
For your name's sake, lead me and guide me (Ps 30:2-3).

The most likely author of this Psalm was David, whose words were fulfilled when recited by the one who was Messiah—the one anointed in an incomparably higher degree than David was an anointed of the Lord.

In the Messiah to come, all pious Jews expected the fulfillment of Psalm 88 celebrating the promises made to David, promises that could be absolutely certain in their outcome because they rested on the stability which Yahweh the Rock was:

I have found David my servant . . .
He will say to me: "You are my father,
my God, the rock who saves me."
And I will make him my firstborn,
the highest of the kings of the earth (Ps 88: 20, 26-27).

It is of minor importance whether David the warrior king composed Psalm 144, an appeal for victory and peace, which starts with the exclamation:

> Blessed be the Lord, my rock,
> who trains my arms for battle,
> who prepares my hands for war! (Ps 144:1)

Such an appeal was always timely in Jewish history and so was the lesson contained in Psalm 93. It warned all men of pride about God, the vindicator of his people, whose spokesman prayed:

> When I think: I have lost my foothold
> your mercy, Lord, holds me up . . .
> As for me the Lord will be a stronghold:
> my God will be the rock where I take refuge (Ps 93:18, 22).

Of course, the Jews could become stiff-necked toward God, an attitude which was pinpointed already, as the clue to Jewish history, in the great farewell of Moses. What happened in the desert cast its shadow over the rest of Jewish history.[19] The water from the rock and the bread from heaven were not enough to bend the stiff-necked. The Lord's vengeance followed and in its wake came sobering reconsiderations. Or as Psalm 77 brought the lesson back to each and every Jew:

> When he slew them then they would seek him,
> return and seek him in earnest.
> They would remember that God was their rock
> God the Most High their redeemer (Ps 77:34-35).

What happened in the desert anticipated the history of salvation. The great interpreters and seers of that history were the prophets, and among them Isaiah was the most historically minded.[20] Whether he saw Israel crushed because of her infidelity to Yahweh, or whether he conjured up her final deliverance, the reference to Yahweh the Rock served as the ultimate reason for the chain of events he foresaw. In Isaiah's oracles about the pagan nations, Damascus becomes the instrument of God's vengeance for the infidelity of his people, all of whose cities will be laid waste:

> For you have forgotten God, your savior,
>   and remembered not the Rock, your strength.
> Therefore, though you plant your pagan plants
>   and set out your foreign vine slips . . .
> Though you make them grow the day you plant them
>   and make your sprouts blossom on the next morning,
> The harvest shall disappear on the day of the
>   grievous blow,
>   the incurable blight (Is 17:10-11).

Since Yahweh decrees a fate as such, its outcome is as firmly set as the firmness of the Rock he is. In predicting Jerusalem's fall,[21] the prophet Habakkuk emphasizes precisely the firmness of divine decisions and does it with a clear reference to Yahweh the Rock:

> Are you not for eternity, Lord
>   my holy God, immortal?
> O Lord, you have marked him [Judah] for judgment.
> O Rock! you have readied him for punishment! (Hab 1:12).

The turmoils caused by the great powers are the anticipation of the apocalyptic consummation of history which the Remnant[22] alone will survive. The pledge of such an unlikely outcome is, according to Isaiah, Yahweh the Rock who cannot fail:

> On that day they will sing this song in the
>   land of Judah:
> "A strong city have we;
>   he sets up walls and ramparts to protect us.
> Open up the gates

> to let in a nation that is just,
>   one that keeps faith.
> A nation of firm purpose you keep in peace;
>   in peace, for its trust [is] in you."
> Trust in the Lord forever!
>   For the Lord is an eternal Rock
> He humbles those in high places
>   and the lofty city he brings down (Is 26:1-4)

Lyrical poetry reached its height a little later as Isaiah portrayed the mood of that day of final deliverance in an image which shows the chosen ones marching toward the mountain of the Lord, to the Rock of Israel:

> You will sing
>   as on a night when a feast is observed,
> And be merry of heart,
>   as one marching along with a flute
> Toward the mountain of the Lord,
>   toward the Rock of Israel,
> accompanied by timbrels and lyres (Is 30:29).

NOTES

[1]Most biblical passages quoted in this chapter are, because of their poetical form, difficult to date with as much exactitude as can be done, say, with distinctly historical passages. But precisely because of their poetical form, the oldest form of articulation, the traditional authorship and dates assigned to them ought not to be taken lightly.

[2]As evidenced, for instance, by the tragic outcome of David's census of Israelites capable of bearing arms. See 2 S 24.

[3]This consideration is the source of confidence which sets the tone of Isaiah's scathing criticism of idolatry. For the far-reaching consequences of that confidence, see my *Science and Creation* (Edinburgh: Scottish Academic Press; New York: Science History Publications, 1974), pp. 155-56

[4]See illustrations in *Dictionary of the Bible* by J. L. McKenzie (New York: Macmillan, 1973), p. 454.

[5]Ibid. and p. 424.

[6]A case in point is the heroic resistance of Jews, withdrawn to the

cliff and fortress of Machaerus, against the Romans for two years after the destruction of Jerusalem.

[7]Not so much by their hostility as by their cultural pressure as evidenced, for instance, in the Israelites' requesting Samuel to appoint a king for them, for "we too must be like other nations . . ."(1 S 8:20).

[8]1 S 4-5.

[9]1 S 16.

[10]For detailed information, see S. Mowinckel, *The Psalms in Israel's Worship* (Oxford: B. Blackwell, 1962).

[11]The principle theme of C. Vagaggini's magisterial treatise, *Il senso teologico della liturgia* (1956), available in English translation, *Theological Dimensions of the Liturgy* (Collegeville, Minn.: The Liturgical Press, 1976).

[12]The rationalist tendency to place most of the Psalms into the Maccabean period has for some time been largely abandoned. See McKenzie, *Dictionary of the Bible,* p. 704.

[13]Moreover, Yahweh is over any and all parts of nature, a feature which raises biblical monotheism to a level incomparably higher than the highest form of worship attained in ancient Egypt during the brief reign of Akhenaton when an exclusive sun-worship was enforced.

[14]The tradition was well attested to by Josephus in his *Jewish Antiquities* (I, 13, 2). See *Josephus,* vol. IV, pp. 111-13.

[15]For a summary of details, see McKenzie, *Dictionary of the Bible,* p. 359.

[16]See Lev 20:2-5; 2 K 23:10; Je 32:35.

[17]The phrase was certainly a commonplace in books written on astronomy and cosmology prior to the 19th century. Its recent comeback, though in a disguised form, can be spotted in Einstein's letter of January 1, 1951, to his friend, M. Solovine. There Einstein warns lest his cosmology be taken as evidence that he had "fallen in the hands of priests."

[18]Perhaps in the company of Saul. See 1 S 15.

[19]This stiff-neckedness seems to qualify more to be the "natural genius" of the Israelites of old in matters religious than the obviously "unnatural" sequence of prophets trying to keep alive their faithfulness to Yahweh. What happened during the long reign of Manasseh (687 B.C. - 642 B.C.), described graphically in 2 K 21 1-17, should seem particularly instructive in this respect. The decades immediately preceding the destruction of Jerusalem in 585 B.C. tell the same story, which is grippingly expanded in F. Werfel's *Hearken unto the Voice,* a historical novel dealing with the life of Jeremiah.

[20]The question of Deutero-Isaiah is irrelevant in this connection.

[21]On the reliability of dating Habakkuk's prophecies to the end of the 7th century B.C., see McKenzie, *Dictionary of the Bible*, p. 329.

[22]The theme of the "remnant" is increasingly strong with the later prophets who obviously speak with an eye on the great historic catastrophes that befell Israel. Not being a "triumphalist" theme, it is rarely found in the writings of some latter-day theologians who, while denouncing old-fashioned triumphalism, try to make Christian faith universally triumph by recasting it according to the dictates of the fashions of the day, a new triumphalism far more counterproductive than the old.

III. A Man Called Rock

Marching toward Yahweh, the Rock, is the meaning and implication of salvation history. The baptism of Christ, marking the beginning of his public ministry, initiated the final phase of that march, and John the Baptizer was the God-appointed witness of that beginning. He not only recognized the Messiah in Christ but also saw the Spirit of God descend upon Jesus in the form of a dove, and heard the heavenly Father's words of approval. But no sooner had Jesus stepped out of the Jordan than John the Baptizer alerted two of his disciples by pointing at Jesus and saying : "Look! There is the Lamb of God!" The two disciples were John and Andrew who needed no further prodding. They immediately started out after Jesus who turned around and asked them: "What are you looking for?" They wanted to know where he was staying. "Come and see," was the answer. Before long they reached Jesus' lodgings where they stayed that day. Staying with them was a third but not explicitly invited guest, Andrew's brother, Simon, who was also in John the Baptizer's entourage and who had been immediately alerted by Andrew who said: "We have found the Messiah." As Andrew brought Simon to Jesus, he looked at him and said: "You are Simon, son of John; your name shall be Cephas (which is rendered Peter" (Jn 1:35-42).

Giving a new name, especially at the very first look, meant a claim on the one who was being named.[1] While the first man could claim to himself all the animals by naming each, he could not claim himself. By receiving his name, Adam, from God, he was claimed by God. So was Eve, the first woman, although Adam was permitted to name her. They were both claimed by God for the role of propagating knowledge and love of him, which also implied a mastery over nature. God claimed Abram for the role of starting the history of salvation by giving him the name Abraham.[2]

The meaning of the name "John" is "Yahweh is gracious." When Zechariah insisted that it be given to his only son, it could only prompt the wonderment implied in the question: "What will this child be?" And an angel from heaven, instructing Mary on what to name her son, was a clear indication of the unique role and status of Jesus. Like the first Adam, the new Adam received his name from God, a name that meant "Yahweh is salvation."[3]

The name was not new and it was most appropriate for a Jew to exclaim, "Yahweh is salvation!" The name "Jesus" was increasingly popular in postexilic times of growing messianic expectations. Ecclesiasticus, one of the last books of the Old Testament, was authored by one Sirach, son of a Jesus, around 190 B.C.[4] Since Jesus came to fulfill the Old Covenant, it was most appropriate for him to carry a name which had been widely used by the constituents of the Old Covenant for at least a dozen or so generations.

The name "Yahweh," He Who Is, which was part of the name "Jesus," was a most sacred, most original, and most appropriate name for the Ultimate in existence and Foundation of all existence. Philosophy itself became perennial, that is, stable, when it became based on what Etienne Gilson aptly called the metaphysics of Exodus,[5] the book which contains Yahweh's revelation about the name most appropriate to him.[6] Existence is the ultimate beyond which no reflection can go. The ultimate ground of existence could only be called Existence, or He Who Is. This is why Yahweh was spoken of as Rock, or immovable foundation, at the great junctures of history.

In view of the implicit presence of God's special name, Yahweh, in various names given to Jews, a name like "Yahweh is my Rock" *(Yah-sur)* would have been quite natural in Jewish context. That such a name was not formed might perhaps have been due to the fact that no Jew was ever called *sur* or Rock. A curious fact since the Jews of old were not reluctant to give descriptive names.[7] Judas and his brothers were quickly called *makkebet* (hammer) once they began to hammer the oppressors of their people.[8] In many vicissitudes of Jewish history not a few acted as if they were a rock, that is, a source of firmness and safety for others. But none of them was given the name Rock, and certainly not in that emphatic manner in which Simon, son of Jonah, was declared Rock by the Son of God.

The only instance of a great Old Testament figure being alluded to as rock is no exception to that pattern. The instance is in that section of Isaiah's prophecies which begins with the description of the Servant of God whose sufferings will alone secure final salvation, a description all too well known from the liturgy of Good Friday. Such a prospect of salvation calls for an unusual measure of trust. It is in his appeal for such trust that Isaiah calls attention to the people's glorious ancestry in which each phase, especially the case of Abraham and Sarah, displays God's power over any and all odds:

> Listen to me you who pursue justice,
>   who seek the Lord;
> Look to the rock from which you were hewn.
>   To the pit from which you were quarried;
> Look to Abraham your father,
>   and to Sarah, who gave you birth
> When he was but one I called him,
>   I blessed him and made him many (Is 51:1-2).

Obviously the rock here symbolizes not strength but barrenness, a condition common to both Abraham and Sarah,
which only God's power could overcome.[9] God's power alone
made possible the bursting of life-giving waters out of the rock
struck by Moses and the same power could, as John the Baptist
warned, call forth children of Abraham out of stone. The devil
was referring to divine power by his suggestion that Jesus
should turn stones into so many fresh loaves of bread. Rock, as
a symbol of barrenness, that could be overcome only by God,
was all too obvious across the whole land and throughout both
Covenants. This is why, to remain within the Old Testament milieu, Isaiah's reference to Abraham (and Sarah) as a rock did not
prompt a portrayal of Abraham as symbolizing strength in the
form of rock in subsequent Old Testament books, although
Abraham was celebrated in them on more than one occasion.[10]
It was not until medieval times that a Talmudic author called
Abraham "Rock," namely, the rock-foundation of the world.[11]
The isolated character of this name and its medieval provenance
suggest that it was born of a defensive tactic. As the papacy
reached its pinnacle of temporal power in the Middle Ages, a
power which was justified all too often with the references to
Jesus' words to Peter,[12] it was most tempting for a Talmudic author to extol Abraham as the true power and foundation.

It is, in itself, possible that the absence in the Old Testament of the word "Rock" as a proper name was a mere accident
and not the result of an instinctive resolve that such a name
ought to be reserved for Yahweh, the only real foundation and
safety. The fact that in the Old Testament God was called
Judge, Father, King, and Lord did not stand in the way of calling mere humans judges, fathers, kings, and lords (gods). Indeed,
Jesus relied on this last point in one of his arguments with the
Pharisees.[13]

The argument was one of the several evidences of Jesus'
consummate skill in quoting the Bible. It is natural to think of
his reading and commenting on Isaiah in the synagogue of

Nazareth in the opening phase of his public ministry,[14] as the first manifestation of that skill, but it was already manifest in the name given by him to Simon. Instead of calling Simon *sur*, he called him *kepha*. The former was the chief biblical word for rock, the latter was the Aramaic version, commonly used in Jesus' time, for the biblical *keph*, which occurs only a few times in the Old Testament.[15]

In view of Jesus' utmost care about theologically crucial words, a care of which more will be said later, it is rather unlikely that he merely followed the routine of Aramaic idiom. The more ancient Hebrew parlance was still alive not only among the learned (Jesus himself astonished the townsfolk of Nazareth by his versatility in the Hebrew Scriptures), but also through the Psalms and other classic prayers known by heart even by the common folk. Through the Psalms the word *sur* was kept alive, and, unexpected as it would be as a name, its meaning would have been readily perceived. Yet to pious Jews such as Andrew, John, and Simon, it would have also become obvious that the name *sur*, when applied to a human, involved an incongruity to which they must have been specially sensitive. The minds of pious Jews were molded by the words of the Psalms which they imbibed at home, in the synagogue, and in the yearly pilgrimage to Jerusalem. For the pilgrims of old the Psalms were the backbone of piety and folklore. The young and the old knew many of the shorter Psalms by heart. One need not be a student of primitive tribes—it is enough to have spent one's younger years as a scout—to realize the ease with which one can learn scores of poems just by singing them. The longer Psalms were at least familiar to anyone attending the Sabbath services in the synagogues. One of the characteristics of the major feasts was the selection of specific Psalms for them.[16]

The Psalms, as already shown, were most emphatic on the point that God was Rock (*sur*); that he was the only Rock; and that this was why he the only one called Rock. As the psalmist put it, common folks were mere breath, and great men but illusions. Had Jesus called Simon *sur* and not *kepha*, Andrew, John and Simon might have sensed something of a blasphemy. Being the disciple of John the Baptizer, all three had the Law and the Prophets as their staple conversation. Even if they did not learn to read the scrolls, they had learned by ear many passages from the Bible.

On hearing Jesus call Simon *kepha*, they were spared sensing a touch of blasphemy in Jesus' words. Yet they could hardly help also sensing the similarity between *sur* and *kepha*.[17] Jesus' choice of *kepha* left Simon what he was, a mere man, while the very same name grafted on him, through its being closely synonymous with *sur*, something superhuman. The coexistence of human and superhuman in Simon was the source of his spiritual drama, a drama to be continued in his often all too human successors.

Certainly, Simon was mere man. When a year or so later Jesus started his march toward Jerusalem, where Yahweh the Rock was present in a special way, to fulfill the eternal plan implied in his name "Yahweh is salvation," it was Simon, already called Rock, who remonstrated.[18] Only a mere man could fail to derive firmness of purpose from the dazzling light in which his Master appeared only a few hours earlier in his transfiguration on the Mountain of Tabor. Simon the Rock was rebuked by being called Satan,[19] a rebuke administered with a firmness that could only come from someone uniquely hewn out of Yahweh, the Rock.

Yet it was Simon called Rock who perceived that Christ was hewn of a divine Rock. He shared not the popular evaluation of Christ as a latter-day Elijah, or Jeremiah, or one of the prophets. To Christ's question—"and you, who do you say that I am?"—Simon, called Rock, answered: "you are the Messiah, the son of the living God." Of that God he knew that he was the Rock of Israel, the everlasting Rock. It is not difficult to guess what Simon must have felt when his name, a pledge of a new reality, was turned by Christ into a most novel and momentous reality as he heard the words which made history. They did so partly because they were cast in an unmistakably Aramaic rhythm[20] which through its genuineness tied those words to a specific hour of history. History was to reverberate from the rhythm of the words:

> Blessed are you, Simon son of Jonah!
> No mere man has revealed this to you,
> but my heavenly Father.
> I for my part declare to you, you are "Rock,"
> and on this rock I will build my church,
> and the jaws[21] of death shall not prevail against it.
>
> (Mt 16:17-18)

In the same breath and with the same unmistakable Aramaic rhythm Jesus also gave the keys of the kingdom of Heaven to that Rock.[22]

Simon was now Rock, the rock foundation of his Master's church, and not merely the carrier of the name "Rock" which the same Master gave him at the moment of their first meeting. The name obviously had a far deeper meaning than *boanerges* (sons of thunder), the name Jesus gave to James and John.[23] While Yahweh thundered, he was never called "thunder" or "thunderer." Only pagan gods could be thunderers (Jupiter was one of them), sources of fright; and never, like a rock, sources of safety. Although the Twelve had their differences and disputes—they all wanted to be the first in the Kingdom of God and they all wanted the best seats there—it is unlikely that they disputed the name *kepha* given to Simon. If it had just been equivalent to "Rocky," it would probably have prompted a joke or some taunt. Being closely synonymous with *sur*, the name *kepha* could not help but evoke in pious Jews, as all the Twelve were, a sentiment of awe and reverence.

Obviously, a name of such connotation could not be the vehicle of that disapproval which lurks behind Jesus' calling James and John *boanerges*.[24] This name, not at all praiseworthy, was for a passing moment, whereas *kepha* was a name to last for the sake of everlasting praise. This everlasting perspective of *kepha* is also suggested by the fact that in spite of having named and made Simon the Rock, Christ kept referring to him as Simon, son of Jonah. Such was Christ's subtle way of making it clear that as long as he was visibly present he alone was the spiritual Rock. Yet, it should seem remarkable that this subtle strategy did not make the others forget that Simon was Rock. While recalling long-past encounters between Christ and Simon, the Evangelists referred to Simon as Cephas without forgetting that Christ had addressed him as Simon.[25] Such is an uncanny evidence of the awareness of the Evangelists that Jesus did not, in a sense, encourage the practice of referring to Simon as Cephas. He left that practice to arise from the spiritual resources of the community of the faithful he was to leave behind as lambs and sheep entrusted to Simon Peter.

Jesus' words turning Simon into Rock were pronounced "in the neighborhood of Caesarea Philippi." This was the area of the headwaters of the Jordan, the sacred river that stopped flowing so that the ark could be carried dry-shod into the promised land. As pious Jews, Jesus and the Twelve could not go right to the spring in that "fathomless" cavity because its very vicinity was exploited for Pan's rites. Those rites brought at times even death to some panic-stricken victims of an idolatry which could readily issue in unbridled debauchery. Such rites were the fearful encroachment of death on the sacred river at its very source, a source which provided the water for Jesus' baptism, the prototype of the rite by which the power of Satan is broken. Standing at a distance, Jesus and the Twelve must have been impressed by the massive wall of rock rising over the source of the Jordan. Here was a sacred river taking its origin through an opening in a massive wall of rock, an opening which could evoke the wide-open jaws of death—both spiritual and physical death. Against this backdrop Jesus spoke to Simon: "You are Rock and on this rock I will build my church, and the jaws of death shall not prevail against it." To echo such words called for a wall of rock.

That such was the background will not appear mere conjecture if one is ready to go by Matthew's instruction, and in disregard of Cullmann's argumentation,[26] to "the neighborhood of Caesarea Philippi" as that very background. It will appear even less of a conjecture if one recalls Jesus' fondness for choosing appropriate backdrops for his words. Jacob's ancient and hallowed well at Sichem heard his words about living waters which only he could give.[27] The feast of Tabernacles with its torches, heard the declaration that he was the light of the world.[28] The ripening harvest heard his urging that the Master of the harvest be asked to send more harvesters into it, for the work to be done was immense in proportion to the number of workers.[29] The little child whom he called over was his visible demonstration to his adult apostles that unless they became like little children they were not to enter the Kingdom of God.[30]

Jesus never did anything without planning. He said only what he wanted. He did only what he intended. His enemies plans could not be fulfilled until *his* hour came.[31] He went to Jerusalem only when it was appropriate for his purposes. His enemies could not lay their hands on him until he handed himself over to them. Neither his enemies, nor his enthusiastic friends could turn him into a messianic king. He called himself the son of Man, the most elusive, the most mysterious of all messianic titles, but also the title most untainted by earthly expectations.[32]

He never attended rabbinical schools, but his mastery of the Law and the Prophets was unparalleled in its simplicity and incisiveness. From the Psalms he could borrow passages—such as the one in which David calls his offspring his master—that left his antagonists gasping for words.[33] He certainly knew that being called Rock (*sur*) was a most sacred privilege of Yahweh through the entire Old Testament. If anyone, he knew what was implied in calling Simon, a mere man, *kepha* or Rock, a word closely synonymous with *sur*. He certainly knew how much more was implied in turning that mere man into the Rock on which he would build his church with a stability that was a sharing in the permanence of Yahweh himself.

Knowing all this, and being "in the neighborhood of Caesarea Philippi," Jesus would not have been faithful to his pedagogy if he had not chosen that massive wall of rock as the backdrop for his historic words "upon this rock."

All his startling statements were somehow anticipated in the Old Testament. The bread from heaven, the love of neighbor, the unconditional love of God, the promise of resurrection, the pouring out of the Spirit of God were themes with clear antecedents in the Old Testament. But no passage intimated that a mere man was ever to be declared *the* Rock. Indeed all the relevant passages seemed to foreclose such eventuality. This is why his words "you are rock" needed a most expressive backdrop.

The thesis that a massive wall of rock with a gaping cave in it was the background of Christ's words to Peter, will forever remain beyond the reach of rigorous proof.[34] What can be rigorously proven is the background voice of the Old Testament. A main purpose of this book is to present that voice in detail, a voice which one would try in vain to find in learned books on Peter, written by biblical scholars.[35] Unless one keeps that voice in mind and unless one recalls its ultimate provenance, one shall never suspect the real meaning of the fact that through the Word of God there is a mere man called and made the Rock.

And what a mere unreliable man he was! What a contrast he was to that absolute permanence which is an essential part of the Rock, that is, Yahweh! Yet Simon's God-given name and Simon's god-decreed reality as Rock made sense only if they embodied somehow the characteristic of permanence in that very sense in which the Church was to be an enduring entity. Simon, the Rock, did not exist for himself but for the Church whose foundation he was to remain forever.

It is not the purpose of this book to unfold that aspect of the Peter-question. One can believe, as Roman Catholics do, in the permanence of a tangible rock in the Church without paying attention to the semantic connection of that rock to Yahweh, the Rock. Christ's words, "you are rock," have their validity even if Yahweh had never been called Rock in the Old Testament.

Yet the voice of the Old Testament is most suggestive and so is the sight of that massive wall of rock "in the neighborhood of Caesarea Philippi." That authors of guidebooks, written for the benefit of pilgrims touring the Holy Land, ignore both, can readily be forgiven. It takes years before the voice of scholarship—which still has to become clear and unanimous concerning that wall—is heard on the popular level. As to the voice of the Old Testament, only a mild surprise is registered here for Cullmann's failure (and for the failure of other biblical scholars) to pay attention to the Old Testament background of his hero's name. Since biblical scholars are known, at times, to be meticulous even about mere molehills, a biblical and archaeological look at a huge rock would hardly have been out of place in a scholarly book on Peter, such as Cullmann's, that was so intent on Bible and archaeology.[36]

Far more useful and constructive than such asides should be a reflection on Peter himself, on the process of his transformation into a Rock. What he thought of being called a Rock and of being declared a Rock is not too difficult to guess. He certainly was a pious and ardent Jew, but he was also a young man with all the superficiality of youth. As a pious Jew, his soul must have resonated with awe at the mere thought of the conceptual analogy between his name and a name reserved for Yahweh. However, it seems that Simon's ardent if not impetuous character derived at first less awe and more self-esteem from his special status. He learned before long that undue self-esteem would easily shatter some illusory aspects of his being the Rock.

For the time being his confidence and self-esteem could only increase. He was the continual recipient of special favors and attention from Jesus. His house in Caphernaum served as Jesus' residence.[37] Jesus used his boat and paid the Temple tax in association with him.[38] Finding the coin equivalent to the tax in the mouth of the first fish he caught should have been less an emboldening experience than a shattering one. He certainly was shattered on seeing the miraculous catch of fish,[39] though he could be bold enough to challenge Jesus to enable him to walk on the water.[40] Not being yet entirely lost in his Master, he might have lost his life right there if not for the merciful understanding of Jesus. Although he was given to witness, while in the company of James and John, such events as the raising of Jairus' daughter, the transfiguration, as well as the agony of Jesus, neither James nor John nor the rest of the Twelve were given the power of the keys. Neither James nor John nor the rest resented him as a leader, although they were all given the power of binding and loosing.[41] He was a leader by nature and by Christ's words. It was his nature that made him a leader of the Twelve when they searched for Jesus after he had retired into the desert to pray.[42] Again, it might have been by the impetuosity of his nature that he was the one to raise important questions about forgiveness and eternal rewards.[43] It was not, however, his nature but Christ's influence that made him a leader at one critical juncture. It was when the crowd, having experienced the miracle of the loaves and fish, nevertheless found the road to Christ the bread too difficult to follow. To the question of Jesus, "Do you want to leave me too?" it was Simon the Rock who answered: "Lord, to whom shall we go? You have the words of eternal life. We have come to believe, we are convinced, that you are God's holy one" (Jn 7:68-69).

It was a magnificent outburst of loyalty, but like other outbursts this too could be without proper depth. Simon the Rock displayed almost childish superficiality when Jesus started washing the feet of his disciples. The attenuating circumstance was his intense love for the Master, but as events were to show very quickly, that love was not yet strong enough to endure unusual strain. He was still to be transformed into that Rock that his Master told him he was.

He boasted that even if all the others were to desert Jesus, he would stand by no matter what.[44] But a little later he could not resist the urge to sleep. In spite of Christ's explicit words he did not suspect the difference between a ready spirit and a weak flesh. On seeing the enemy come, he acted as man of outbursts. He drew his sword and drew blood. His Master was not impressed: he healed the bleeding ear of Malchus, the high priest's servant, on the spot.

But Jesus was very much interested when Peter, the boasting and sword-rattling leader of the Twelve, was forced into a triple betrayal triggered by the wagging tongue of a servant girl.[45] As a self-centered enthusiast, Peter needed an outside reminder to perceive his true predicament. It came when Jesus turned around and looked at him as the cock crowed. Peter wept bitterly as he went out of the courtyard where he had just seen the Messiah passing through, rejected and humiliated by his own.

Convulsive tears could be produced by a deep love which did not turn into disillusion when the beloved Master utterly failed by all human standards. His dead body was now the last link Peter had with him. A strong link it was. When told on early Easter morning that the tomb was empty, he rushed there with John who, although first in the race, deferred to him in the moment of victory. Peter entered the tomb first, a possible deference to his leadership.[46] Since he did not expect Jesus to rise from the dead, he must have felt heartbroken on seeing that the dead body of his Master, his last link with him, had vanished. Being by nature an intense lover, he could only go outside the tomb and weep.

Legend has it that Peter often wept for the rest of his life and that the tears made deep furrows in his cheeks. But a few, hardly visible, sincere tears were enough to turn Peter into a rock through which the marvel of grace made living waters

flow, as was the case with the rock in the desert struck by
Moses. That rock, as Saint Paul emphatically remarked, prefig-
ured Christ,[47] who when hanging on the cross let the Church be
born in the water and blood that flowed from his pierced
heart.[48] The rock, which was to be the continuation of Christ,
also had to be a source of the water of life-giving suffering.

In order to assure that continuity, Jesus, through some
heartrending questions, caused Peter to cry. When Peter rushed
through the water after spotting Jesus on the shore, he did not
realize what was in store for him. A rock-like stability was to be
grafted on his nature, which had been shaken by outbursts of
emotions. Grafts always extract some moisture, and there must
have been some tears in Peter's eyes when his Master asked him
for the third time: "Do you love me more than these?" The
proof of the tears is Peter's answer, given as he trembled in
pain, "Lord, you know everything. You know well that I love
you," the kind of answer that can hardly be made without tears
in one's eyes. In reply Jesus let him hear for the third time, the
biblical symbol of consummation, his great assignment: "Feed
my lambs, feed my sheep."[49] He already had the keys of the
kingdom; he now received the staff of the supreme shepherd.

What immediately followed showed that Peter had under-
gone a momentous change. He did not remonstrate when Christ
conjured up for him an old age fearfully different from his
younger days, when he could come and go as he liked. Some-
time in the future others would come, make him stretch out his
hands, tie him fast and carry him against his very wish. John,
the Evangelist, who heard these words, many years later remarked: "What Christ said indicated the sort of death by which
Peter was to glorify God" (Jn 21:19). Peter's crucifixion came
only some thirty years later, but he came very close to martyrdom within a year or two. His being flogged and thrown into
prison by Herod, who decided to execute him to please the
Jews, and his miraculous escape are described in graphic details
in the Acts of the Apostles. The story shows a new Peter, with

no trace of outbursts of self-confidence, a man completely composed, with his confidence centered on God the Rock. During those dark days the whole Church constantly prayed for him and Peter prayed without ceasing. His prayers could only be the Psalms, most of which he knew by heart (his speeches, recorded in the Acts, are full of quotations from the Psalms). For one destined to execution no Psalms could be more appropriate than Psalms 93 and 30. The former was, as already shown, a prayer to God the Rock, the Judge and Vindicator. The latter was a prayer in ultimate distress, a prayer full of confidence in a God who was Rock itself.

No talent for dramatization is needed to read those Psalms and see how they found their fulfillment as they became the source of strength for Simon the Rock when he was in the death row. Without straining the imagination, one can be sure that following his miraculous escape, Simon the Rock instinctively turned to Psalm 91, a jubilation in the saving strength of Yahweh the Rock. The one who had already discouraged Cornelius from genuflecting before him with the words—"I am only a man myself"[50]—must have known in full that his endurance as a rock was a mirage unless maintained by Yahweh the Rock.

Almost immediately afterwards, Peter left Jerusalem for good. For the rest of his life he was in exile, first in Antioch and later in Rome, the Great Babylon. For an exile no Psalm was better suited than Psalm 41, especially for someone who had been made *the* Rock at the very foot of Mount Hermon. The Psalm brought him back to the first cataracts of the Jordan, bubbling forth from that massive wall of rock, the backdrop of the history-making words addressed to him. He was now making that history, the history of the new Jerusalem which was not of the flesh but of the spirit, not of ordinary stones but, as he wrote in his First Letter, "of living stones, built as an edifice of spirit into a holy priesthood, offering spiritual sacrifices acceptable to God through Jesus Christ" (1 Pt 2:4).

The edifice was a temple of which he was the Supreme Pontiff but wholly unlike the Pontifex Maximus of the Romans. Unlike that Pontifex, who was at best feared, Peter was intensely liked by his associates in faith. This was his only distinction. For Imperial Rome he was but one of the "common folks" —"only a breath," to recall the words of Psalm 61. Peter could see daily the lighthearted waste of human lives, as if so many breaths, in a pagan milieu intent on the pride of life and the desires of the flesh.

But he could also see that great men, to recall the same Psalm again, were only "illusions." The proof was their quick succession. In such a context, life was highly precarious and the only strength was, to recall the same Psalm, Yahweh the Rock. The words of that Psalm never sounded more genuine than on the lips of Simon the Rock carrying out humbly his historic task in the shadow of a huge rock, called Capitoline, the seat of the Roman Empire and a supreme symbol of the "jaws of death" for the first Christian generations.

Yet those Christians never rebelled. They remembered not only Christ's command to love one's enemies—a supreme form of endurance—but also Peter's urging that they should "foster respect for the emperor."[51] The manner he chose for his martyrdom—to be crucified with his head down out of respect for his Master—spoke better than words about the sincerity concerning that respect and about the measure of his endurance.

It is not known whether prior to his crucifixion Peter was kept in a prison cave, at the foot of the Capitoline. The prison literally served as the jaws of death for many Christians and symbolically enough was found at the foot of a huge rock. Peter was already in the safety of heaven when the legions of Titus marched to the Capitoline carrying the sacred vessels from the Temple of Jerusalem, where in fulfillment of Jesus' words no stone was left upon stone.[52] The truly perfect Temple of Yahweh, as Jesus hinted to the Samaritan woman,[53] was not to be built on a physical rock however prominent and hallowed by tradition, but on a spiritual rock whose enduring strength was the endurance of trials, including martyrdom. For as Jesus said, no disciple was greater than his master and the truth of this had to be especially valid for the one whose name invariably stood at the head of the list of the twelve disciples.

Matthias was added to that list by lot to fill the place vacated by Judas. The other addition, Paul of Tarsus, was made by a special act of God. Like all "acts of God," Paul too was spectacular. In a sense he eclipsed any and all the disciples, but only in a sense which meant no rivalry. Symbolically enough, his earthly life eclipsed in close connection with that of Peter. Such was the God-decreed proof that Paul invited no rebellion against Simon the Rock when he took exception to Simon's policy as to what was prudent in such a practical matter as the attitude toward food declared unclean by Mosaic Law.[54] In addition to this symbolic detail, Peter's reverential reference in his Second Letter to "our dear brother Paul" and to his God-given wisdom,[55] also carries us into a milieu made divine by the wisdom of a life that had matured in the message of the cross.

In an age when life-expectancy hardly exceeded thirty years, Peter and Paul, both sixtyish, could rightly look upon themselves with the words of Psalm 70, as old and grey-headed. The same Psalm was more than appropriate for both, as they marched, one to beheading, the other to crucifixion. They died at opposite ends of Rome, but they were united in spirit and in the words of Psalm 70 which old and grey-headed Jews prayed in ultimate distress.

Coming as they did from deeply pious Jewish families, it was true of both that, in the words of that Psalm, the Lord was their trust from their youth, that from their mother's womb he was their help, and that he was the one who taught them from their youth. Being in the hand of the wicked, in the grasp of the unjust oppressor, they could only pray:

Be a rock where I can take refuge,
a mighty stronghold to save me;
for you are my rock, my stronghold (Ps 70:3).

NOTES

[1]This is stated with particular explicitness concerning Israel (Is 43:1 and 48:1), Moses (Ex 33:12), and the stars (Is 40:26).

[2]Similarly, the change of Jacob to Israel (Gn 35:10).

[3]Jesus is the late Aramaic form of Joshua, a name which owes its origin to Moses' decision (Nm 13:16) to change Hosea (salvation) into Joshua (Yahweh is salvation).

[4]Until 1896, when two-thirds of the original Hebrew text were discovered in the synagogue of Cairo, the book's earliest form was its Greek translation made by the grandson of Jesus in Egypt in 132 B.C. The book is one of the deuterocanonical books.

[5]The metaphysics in question is all the more profound because it is not conveyed in its jargon. Or as Gilson put it: "No hint of metaphysics, but God speaks, *causa finita est,* and Exodus lays down the principle from which henceforth the whole of Christian philosophy will be suspended." *The Spirit of Medieval Philosophy*, translated by A. H. C. Downes (New York: Charles Scribner's Sons, 1936), p. 51.

[6]"But," said Moses to God, "when I go to the Israelites and say to them, 'The God of your fathers has sent me to you,' if they ask me 'What is his name?' what am I to tell them?" God replied, "I am who am." Then he added, "This is what you shall tell the Israelites: I AM sent me to you." (Ex 3:13-14).

[7]Thus, for instance, Barak (lightning), Deborah (bee), Rachel (ewe).

[8]1 Mc 2:4.

[9]See "Rock" in Xavier-Léon Dufour, *Vocabulaire de théologie biblique* (Paris: Cerf, 1966, cols. 941-42). The symbolism of rock as barrenness in connection with this passage of Isaiah remained curiously overlooked by first-rate Protestant commentators invoked by Cullmann (See *Peter* [1953], p. 186, and [1962], p. 193), all of whom seem to have been burdened by their eagerness to weaken the uniqueness of Peter as rock. Cullmann's reference to Is 53 instead of Is 51 (where, incidentally, the word *sur* is used), is perhaps an indication that he failed to study carefully this particular detail, a point further illustrated by his uncritical reporting of the rabbinical interpretation of that passage. See on this note 11.

[10]The passage on Abraham in Ecclesiasticus (44:19-21) is particularly

revealing for its failure to praise Abraham as a rock (solidity).

[11]The passage from Jalqut (1, 766), "When God looked on Abraham, who was to appear, he said: Behold I have found a rock on which I can build and base the world. Therefore he called Abraham a rock," first received wide publicity through the famous commentary on the Gospel of Matthew by H. L. Strack and P. Billerbeck in the light of passages from Talmud and Midrash (Munich: Beck, 1922, p. 733), and later through Cullmann's *Peter* (1953, p. 186 and 1962, p. 193) and his article "*petra*" in Kittel's *Theological Dictionary of the New Testament* (vol. VI, pp. 95-99). What Cullmann (and Strack and Billerbeck) failed to point out is the fact that the earliest parts of Jalqut, a compilation by Simeon Kara (12th century) of Midrash fragments, are from the 5th century! Actually, the earliest of half a dozen other Talmudic texts describing Abraham as rock, mentioned by Strack and Billerbeck, are from the middle of the second century A.D. Once this is kept in mind, it will be easy to spot the propagandistic over-simplification in the widely available and beautifully illustrated *In the Footsteps of Jesus* written by Wolfgang A. Pax and edited by Mordecai Raannan (Jerusalem: Steimatzky's Agency, 1970; tenth printing, May, 1976) in which one finds, in addition to a photo of the niches at Banias (p. 113), the flat and undocumented declaration: "As Abraham is the rock upon which God built the world, so Peter is the foundation upon which Jesus builds his church" (p. 141).

[12]See Y. Congar, *L'Eglise: De Saint Augustin à l'époque moderne* (Paris: Cerf, 1970), pp. 252-63.

[13]Jn 10:34-35.

[14]Lk 4:17-19.

[15]See Je 4:29 and Jb 30:6.

[16]See note 10 to Chapter II.

[17]Clearly, in the absence of such a similarity, the rendering of *sur* and *kepha* by the same word—rock, *rocher, Fels,* etc.—in the best modern-language translations of the Bible would be wholly unjustified. The difference between *sur* and *kepha* is certainly not that between a huge cliff and a pebble! This is why one finds in the notes of Cullmann's article "*petra*" (see note 11 above), one line which informs the reader with references to Dt, S, Is, and Hb (the Psalms are entirely ignored) that in the Old Testament God is called Rock.

[18]Mk 8:32.

[19]That this detail is reported only in the Gospel of Mark (8:33) reveals something of Peter's humility, because according to an early tradition Mark's Gospel is a summary of Peter's preaching.

[20]As emphatically noted by J. Jeremias, *Golgotha*, pp. 69-70, and by

J.-M. Lagrange, *Evangile selon Saint Matthieu*, p. 321.

[21]The departure in the *New American Bible* from the customary translation of *pulai* (gates) with jaws may seem daring, if not arbitrary. Yet the "gates of hell" readily evoke a gaping entrance to it, an image which the word "jaws" renders vividly also with respect to the strength implied in "gates" as the strongest section in the walls of a fortified city.

[22]In the Old Testament the key is the symbol of the authority of the master of the palace (Is 22:22) and in the extrabiblical Second Book of Baruch the archangel Michael is described as holding the keys of the kingdom of heaven (11:2). In the New Testament Christ speaks disparagingly of the lawyers who keep to themselves the key of knowledge (Lk 11:52) and of the pharisees and scribes who close the kingdom of heaven (Mt 23:13) lest others enter there. For further discussion, see ch II of my book, *The Keys of the Kingdom: A Tool's Witness to Truth* (Chicago, Ill.: Franciscan Herald Press, 1986).

[23]Mk 3:17.

[24]See the parallel passage (Lk 9:54), where James and John want to call down fire upon the inhospitable Samaritans.

[25]The Jewish scholar, Cecil Roth of Oxford, ignored this point in his effort ("Simon-Peter," *Harvard Theological Review* 54 [1961], pp. 91-97) to make it appear that the appellation "Peter" prevailed as time went on over Simon because Jews of the first century, for political reasons, avoided referring to anyone as Simon though given that name at birth. Roth's effort was shown to lack solid basis by J. A. Fitzmyer ("The Name Simon," ibid., 56 [1963], pp. 1-5), who also hinted that in Roth's case too, Jesus' words to Peter apparently formed a thorn in the side.

[26]Cullmann, who removed Christ's words to Peter from the "neighborhood of Caesarea Philippi" to the Last Supper as a "spiritual context" more fitting the prediction of his passion, was duly criticized by B. Willaert ("La connexion littéraire entre la première prédiction de la passion et la confession de Pierre chez les Synoptiques," in *Ephem. Theol. Lov.* 32 [1956], pp. 24-45). As to Cullmann's treatment of the "geographical context," it is puzzling to say the least. For if it is true, as he admits, that the verses Mt 16:17-19 "stand in a setting entirely suitable to them" (*Peter* [1953] p. 179 and [1962] p. 185), then would it not have been required by scholarship to review that setting, rather than escape its demonstrative value by a mere reference to Immisch's article? Again, since Cullmann was reminded by M. Overney in some detail, and with a reference to Immisch's article, of the geographic context of Christ's words to Peter ("Le cadre historique des paroles de

Jésus sur la primauté de Pierre," *Nova et Vetera* 28 [1953], pp. 206-29, see especially pp. 223-24), would it not have been proper on Cullmann's part to come to grips with Overney's essay in the second edition of *Peter* instead of merely referring to it?

[27]Jn 4:4-15.

[28]Jn 8:12. As reported by McKenzie in his *Dictionary of the Bible* (p. 864), the Temple area was, according to the Talmud, brightly lit up by torches on the first day of that feast.

[29]Mt 9:37-38.

[30]Mt 18:2, Mk 10:15, Lk 18:17.

[31]Jn 7:30, 8:20, 12:23.

[32]For an excellent summary, see McKenzie, *Dictionary of the Bible*, pp. 831-33.

[33]Mt 22:41-45.

[34]This, however, does not justify the patent ambivalence in *Jesus and his Times* by Daniel-Rops (Garden-City, N.Y.: Doubleday, 1958), vol. I, pp. 272-73, with respect to the setting of Jesus' words to Peter.

[35]The first fairly explicit treatment of that voice was given in *Simon Pierre rocher biblique* (see note 14 to chapter I) by Ridolfi, a Catholic priest, but not a biblical scholar. Compared with that treatment, the ones in Jeremias' *Golgotha*, in Cullmann's *Peter*, and in his articles *"petra"* and *"Petros"* in Kittel's *Theological Dictionary* seem very unsatisfactory.

[36]Clearly, if Cullmann could devote so many pages in his *Peter* to the archeological evidence concerning Peter's sojourn in Rome, Peter's stay at Caesarea Philippi should have deserved at least a paragraph or two.

[37]The first archeological evidence was obtained through the excavations conducted by Father Gaudenzio Orfali in 1921. For that evidence and for corroborating details obtained during the excavations made in 1968, see *New Memoirs of Saint Peter by the Sea of Galilee*, translated from the Italian by G. Bushell (Jerusalem: Franciscan Printing Press, 1969), with many illustrations and diagrams. See especially, pp. 7-38.

[38]Mt 17:27.

[39]Lk 5:8.

[40]Mt 14:28-31.

[41]Mt 18:18.

[42]Mk 1:36.

[43]Mt 18:21.

[44]Mt 26:33.

[45]Mt 27:69-74.

[46]Jn 20:6. To a modern mind insensitive to intrinsic evidence and

riveted on opinion polls, there ought to be some food for thought in the fact that while Simon Peter is mentioned 195 times in the New Testament, all other apostles receive only 130 mentions with John being the highest among them with 29. See the tables compiled in Appendix A in *The New Testament Witness to Saint Peter* by V. J. McNabb (New York: Benzinger, 1928)

[47]1 Cor 10:4.

[48]For the patristic origins of this, see documentation by S. Tromp to the Encyclical *Mystici corporis* in *Textus et documenta,* Series theologica 26 (Rome: Gregorian University, 1943), pp. 87-88.

[49]A contraction from Jn 21:15-17.

[50]AA 10:26.

[51]1 Pt 2:17.

[52]Lk 19:44.

[53]Jn 4:21.

[54]Had Cephas not been so very important, there would have been no reason for Paul to take as strong a stand as he did.

[55]2 Pt 3:15.

IV. The Shadow of the Rock

If it is appropriate to conclude the story of a man called Rock with the words of one of the Psalms proclaiming God the Rock, one may also start reflections on that story with the words of the same Psalm. In it the "old and grey-headed" speaks of his being the object of his enemies' remark: "God has forsaken him: follow him, seize him, there is not one to save him" (Ps 70:11).

Words like these have often been repeated by enemies of the Church and especially of the Rock on which she is built. The almost two-thousand-year history of the Church offered more than a few opportunities, nay, some apparently good reasons, for uttering such words. Time and again it looked as if the days of the Church, and in particular the days of the papacy, were numbered.[1]

One such time was the second half of the fourth century when Arianism experienced a sudden and vigorous comeback. This return was partially caused by the fact that the Council of Nicea, which had been called to combat Arianism, did not rely exclusively on a supernatural strength. The Council had been called by a Roman emperor, the representative of the natural power of a huge empire, and therefore enjoyed distinctly natural favors.

93

This dependency on natural favors is possibly the reason that the Council was not strong enough to put an immediate end to the subtle strategy of Arius which gained strength from falling back on what is natural. Its lure touched off a flood so vast as to engulf the majority of the bishops as the century drew to a close.

The situation made St. Jerome groan in despair. For comfort he turned to the bishop of Rome, Pope Damasus, the only Rock in sight.

> Yet, though your greatness terrifies me, your kindness attracts me. From the priest I demanded the safe-keeping of the victim, from the shepherd the protection due to the sheep. Away with all that is overweening; let the state of Roman majesty withdraw. My words are spoken to the successor of the fisherman, the disciple of the cross. As I follow no leader save Christ, so I communicate with none but your blessedness, that is, with the chair of Peter. For this, I know, is the Rock on which the church is built. This is the house where alone the paschal lamb can be rightly eaten. This is the ark of Noah, and he who is not found in it shall perish when the flood prevails.[2]

Whatever the strength of Pope Damasus, it was hardly of a political worldly kind. Yet as Jerome remarked, the memories of the power of the established religion of Imperial Rome were already alluring to a papacy that in its first two-hundred-fifty years derived its strength from the weakness of a cross meaning martyrdom. As time went on, many a pope found enjoyment in a strength which was not spiritual,[3] a strength rather illusory and certainly detrimental to the cause his office represented. Even in the last hundred years the strength of the papacy has been a curious mixture of the worldly and the otherworldly. The end of the Papal States a hundred years ago did not mean the abrupt end to the wielding of worldly power by the papacy. Nor was the beginning of that end abrupt. As John Henry Newman, not yet a Cardinal, noted in a letter on December 12,

1870: "The Pope's fall is not abrupt—everyone with eyes in his head must have been sure that it must come—and, even though there be some reaction soon, it won't last—he will gradually lose his power—nor perhaps is it possible in the disposition of Providence that the same man should be both infallible in spirituals and absolute in temporals. The definition of July involved the dethronement of September."[4]

As for infallibility, proclaimed in July 1870, let it be first recalled that a Secretary of the World Council of Churches could declare without tongue in cheek that Pope Paul VI did signal service to the cause of unity when he voiced the spiritual claim of his office during his historic visit to Geneva. He voiced that claim by introducing himself, on June 10, 1969, with the words: "Our name is Peter."[5] These words provoked respect and not angry protests, indicating that responsible Christian voices other than Roman Catholic do not necessarily agree with those Roman Catholics who argue that papal infallibility is an insuperable hindrance to unity,[6] that Vatican I was "rigged,"[7] and that a truly ecumenical council is intrinsically superior to the papacy.[8]

A much more subtle, and therefore serious, hindrance to unity is a presentation of papal infallibility which is aimed at discrediting its essence by dwelling on trivia, whether historical or personal. Such a presentation, behind which lurks a long-outmoded branch-theory of the Church, denies survival to the Roman Catholic communion, and is therefore contradictory. Architects of such a presentation might as well recall that in the immediate wake of the declaration of infallibility, some expected Newman to part with Rome and return to the Anglican communion. In reply he noted that by converting to Rome "I did not hope or long for any 'peace or satisfaction' . . . for any illumination or success. I did not hope or long for anything except to do God's will, which I feared not to do. . . . I did not leave the Anglican Church, as you think, for any scandals in it. . . . Then again, whether I have, since a Catholic, been treated well or ill, by high personages or confidential friends, does not touch the question of truth and error, the Church and schism."[9]

Actually, infallibility is coming into its own in the measure in which the papacy disowns worldly power, a process accelerated by the complete secularization, if not sheer paganization, of life, a process now increasingly apparent. This paganization is not so much the yielding to pagan urges ever present in each and every man, including Christians, but is rather the growing readiness among Christians, Catholic as well as non-Catholic, to dilute Christian norms of faith, and especially of morals, into rules of pagan conveniences.

The heart of Christian unity was indeed touched by the words of Cardinal Willebrands, a universally admired promoter of Christian unity. He warned during his visit at Princeton Theological Seminary on November 25, 1974, that while dogmatic differences among the main Christian communions may no longer appear unbridgeable, a very serious chasm is opening in their midst concerning matters of morals.[10]

For putting himself on the record with the utmost seriousness, responsibility, and clarity on one such matter, Pope Paul has been the target of much resentment within the Christian fold [11] and of violent abuse without.[12] Those within and without should have noticed that our own virulently anti-papal times are becoming the fulfillment of George Bernard Shaw's vision of an infallible pope on his knees. The vision is found in the Preface of Shaw's *Saint Joan* where it is of a merely trivial instructiveness that Joan's excommunication by a provincial ecclesiastical court is admitted to be "not one of the acts for which the Church claims infallibility." The prophetically instructive vision is in Shaw's remark that the pope's infallibility in raising Joan to sainthood was

> by far the most modest pretension of the kind in existence. Compared to our infallible democracies, our infallible medical councils, our infallible astronomers, our infallible judges, and our infallible parliaments, the Pope is on his

knees in the dust confessing his ignorance before the throne of God, asking only that as to certain historical matters on which he has clearly more sources of information open to him than anyone else, his decision shall be taken as final. The Church may and perhaps someday will canonize Galileo without compromising such infallibility as it claims for the Pope, if not without compromising the infallibility claimed for the Book of Joshua by simple souls—whose rational faith in more important things has become bound up with a quite irrational faith in the chronicle of Joshua's campaign as a treatise on physics. Therefore the Church will probably not canonize Galileo yet awhile, though it might do worse. But it has been able to canonize Joan without any compromise at all. She never doubted that the sun went around the earth; she had seen it do so all too often.[13]

While newspapers, dictators, parliaments, scientists, and artists poured derision on Paul VI, he was literally on his knees before his separated brethren, as he kissed the feet of an official delegate of Eastern Orthodoxy,[14] begging forgiveness for his own sundry fallibilities and those of his predecessors. He let years of prayers and fasting precede his major decisions, while carping critics saw those years as evidence justifying the doubtful security of their doubts. Those critics, as do most critics, speak in a manner which suggests a position of strength. Judging by their tone and sweeping dicta, they speak in a patently upright posture. But who was not tempted to stand proudly erect when invited by *The Economist* to write an evaluation, in the form of a cover story, of the aging Paul and of the immediate future of the papacy? Norman St. John-Stivas, author of that article, failed to suspect the irony as he declared by way of a grand and infallibly-sounding conclusion that Rome must stoop in order to conquer.[15]

The vocal strength and upright posture of such critics have a curiously weak foundation in that biblical theology which they like to take for their stronghold. Actually, a brief though realis-

tic glimpse of Peter's inner physiognomy, so easy to grasp from
plain texts, is enough to make one realize how weak their biblical vision is. Not much stronger is their literary memory. After
all, Chesterton's *Heretics*, originally published in 1905, was still
bringing, through its reprints in the 1950's, an age-old lesson in
self-analysis within easy reach of the present generation of
the papacy's ever-young critics:

> When Christ at a symbolic moment was establishing His
> great society, he chose for its cornerstone neither the bril-
> liant Paul nor the mystic John, but a shuffler, a snob, a
> coward—in a word, a man. And upon this rock he has
> built His Church, and the gates of Hell have not prevailed
> against it. All the empires and the kingdoms have failed,
> because of this inherent and continual weakness, that they
> were founded by strong men and upon strong men. But
> this one thing, the historic Christian Church, was founded
> on a weak man, and for that reason it is indestructible. For
> no chain is stronger than its weakest link.[16]

The most prideful and therefore the most universally human element—or link—in the Church is a many-faced self-righteousness, all too ready to criticize the shepherd and cast the
first stone at him. The most humbling and therefore the most
divine characteristic of the "weakest link" in the Church is long-
suffering, a divinely allotted share of shepherd as well as of
sheep. A long-suffering pope is the true strength of the Rock he
is. That strength will be sensed only by those ready to share in
his lengthy trials, none more trying than the deliberate spreading of disloyalty among the sheep.

    Those who spread such disloyalty always claim a cause and
not rarely an apparently just one. Indeed, as history has shown,
the justness of the cause can be as glaring as plain unjustness
and even depravity in the shepherd. Yet it remains just as true
that if hatred can only be corrected by love—and on no other
point is the light of the Gospel so clear and sharp—then it can
be safely assumed that whatever vice can be found in the shep-

herd can only be corrected by the corresponding virtue in the sheep. It is still to be demonstrated that the strategy of spreading disloyalty—be it for a just cause—is a virtue; unless, of course, one accepts it as proven that the end justifies the means.[17]

Long-suffering can, on the other hand, be taken for "failure of nerve" by those "loyal" among the sheep who still dream about a powerful Church that can extend, à la Joshua, the duration of sunlight for a quick completion of the battle, unmindful of its never-ending character. The strength of one's nerves is never proven better than under the stress of trial, which can take on historic dimensions, as described thirty-five years ago by a non-Catholic and certainly not a "triumphalist" Christian:

> . . . the Roman Church, *tam antiqua et tam nova*, haunted by many recurring conflicts and crises, skilled in statesmanship, enriched by an unfathomable memory, is a vigilant Mother-Confessor and a wise Director of Souls. A candid Protestant, or an honest humanist will find himself at least asking—what, in a world rocking in helpless indecision and revealing ominous cracks of threatened collapse, will become of our Christian heritage and traditional culture should that Church compromise its sense of divine commission or if, bribed or tortured by lust of power, it should tremble to impose its own discipline, lose its nerve and snap under breaking strain?[18]

Whether the present is pregnant with such a prospect only history will tell. The past has certainly shown that the only power that can make the Church powerless is lust for power, a temptation to which laymen, priests, *and* theologians are not less prone than bishops and popes. The most subversive type of that lust is not its crudest kind. Dialogue is anything but a crude act. But it can be a vehicle not only of brotherhood but also of reaching out for power by those who mistakenly feel themselves excluded from the sharing of power and turn their dialogue with those in authority into filibuster. Again, opening to the world may not only be a sign of unfettered apostolic zeal, but also of a weak-kneed faith in search of compensations in the cravings of a nature which has the world for its natural ally. Men of little faith are all too ready to declare such cravings legitimate, because they are unable to live with the experience of a constant need for God's redeeming mercy in the face of the continual weakness of a proud nature—an experience endured only by strong faith.

Modern times are, no less than ages long past, a clear evidence of man's perennial reluctance to find strength in the weakness of the cross, a reluctance which is to be kept in check at all times. Catholics, who try to overcome their dissatisfaction with a papacy that is unyielding on crucial issues, by merging themselves into a conciliar euphoria, seem to forget that Vatican II will form no exception to a general characteristic of all previous Councils. They all, and not only the Council of Trent and Vatican I, were the one-sided products of always one-sided times. Paul VI himself spoke in that vein of Vatican II.

To look at Vatican II as a one-sided Council may seem startling in view of that Council's determination not to be lopsided. In many respects the documents of Vatican II show an exemplary balance which any age may envy, but those documents easily lend themselves, precisely because of their balance, to unbalanced interpretations at a time which is notoriously off balance in its cravings and perspectives. The letter addressed to the Council Fathers "from higher authority" was a move to forestall a special danger of one-sidedness which is as strong today as it was some years ago when the keys of Peter seemed to some to be breaking into pieces.

The temptation to tilt the balance, a temptation which unfortunately goes on unabated in the name of Vatican II, is nowhere more crucial than in respect to power and authority in the Church. This is not to suggest that the documents of Vatican II aim, however slightly, at slighting the scandal of the cross. But

with respect to that scandal, every balancing is to tilt the balance toward a nature unreceptive to suffering. Nature without
the cross is the most gravely weakened nature, one which can
feel no sympathy for a Rock whose strength comes from re-
demptive suffering. This point is still to be pondered by two
groups, very different in outlook and expectation. Triumphalist
Catholics, so hopeful about the impact of the personality of
John Paul II, should have, in view of the almost fatal shooting
in St. Peter's square on a May 13 (a day hallowed by the first
apparition at Fatima), ample food for thought about the in-
evitability of the Cross. The Pope himself was all too candid in
crediting Divine Providence not only with his escape from the
jaws of death, but also with the vivid, existential insight given to
him by that incident into that paramount role of suffering in
the life of the Church. On leaving the Gemelli Hospital for the
second time on August 14, John Paul addressed the patients and
the personnel in the following words:

> In giving thanks for His gifts of preserved life and restored
> health, I wish at this time to express thanks for yet another
> thing: in fact, it has been granted to me in the course of
> these three months, dear brothers and sisters, to belong to
> your community: to the holy community of the sick who
> are suffering in this hospital—and, as a matter of fact, who
> constitute in a certain sense a special organism in the
> Church, in the Mystical Body of Christ. . . . In the course of
> these months, it was granted me to belong to this special
> organism . . . I now know better than ever that suffering is
> a certain dimension of life, in which more than ever the
> grace of redemption is deeply engrafted in the human
> heart. And if I wish each one of you to be able to leave
> this hospital restored to health, I no less intensely wish that
> you will be able to take from here also that deep grafting
> of that divine life which the grace of suffering brings with
> it.

The importance which John Paul II attributes to this experience of his can also be gathered from the address which he

gave to the faithful gathered for general audience at St. Peter's Square on October 7th, the first audience of its kind since the day of that infamous shooting. He centered his entire address on the attempt by Herod made at Peter's life and on the prayers of the members of a suffering Church offered on behalf of the shepherd.

As to the self-styled liberals, who stand proudly erect while directing their barrage of criticism at popes on their knees, events of the last ten years provided them with much to reflect upon. They should realize that the destiny of the Church cannot be surmised from journalistic wisdom. Contrary to their diagnosis, the apparently weak posture of Paul VI was anything but a sign of a weakened papacy. The rapidity of the conclaves, which gave us John Paul I and John Paul II, revealed all too well a strength characteristic of undiminished sense of purpose and identity. Those liberals have, of course, been deprived through the election of Cardinal Wojtyla, a man of robust personality, of the advantages of their dubious tactic, their presentation of a long-suffering Paul VI as a man of fumbling. In their disarray, those liberals already look back wistfully to the days of Paul VI as "dialogue" and "humility," a rather transparent effort to discredit John Paul II. They still have to admit that those days were days of strength. Paul VI was indeed so strong as to feel no need to make public a letter written to him by Karl Barth two months before his death in December 1968, just at a time when the attack of liberals (believers and unbelievers) on the author of *Humanae vitae* began to blare forth in fortissimo. In that letter Karl Barth expressed not only his agreement with the position taken in *Humanae vitae* but also commended, of all things, the Pope's heroism: "You may be sure of my great respect for what might be called the heroic isolation in which, Holy Father, you now find yourself."[19]

The isolation of the Pope was not, of course, an isolation from the faithful. Long before the Church was forced to deprive the author of *Infallible?* and of other no less revealing books,[20] of the status of "Roman Catholic theologian," the faithful well perceived that unorthodox stance produces its own isolation. The same is true of the kind of scheming which trapped recently a vocal reformer busy to secure, in the expectation of John Paul II's rapid death, the election of a "liberal" Cardinal through the presumed good services of an archbishop still to make the Sacred College.[21] Beneath all such stances and schemings, invariably strange to the atmosphere of the *prie-dieu*, there lies the inability to perceive that kneeling, the lowest of all stances, casts the longest shadow. Christ demonstrated this as he knelt in the garden of Gethsemani. The length of that shadow is commensurate with its perennial endurance. This in turn is the sole privilege of a Rock destined to cast its warning and protective shadow over all seasons and ages.

NOTES

[1]One such time was the period covered by the younger years of Eneas Silvio de' Piccolomini (1405-64), who later as Pope Pius II (1458-64) felt impelled to disavow most of his previous literary works and especially his earlier way of life, in an Apostolic Letter the gist of which was: "Reject Eneas, hold fast to Pius."

[2]Letter written in 376 or 377. See *Select Library of Nicene and Post-Nicene Fathers* vol. VI, p. 18.

[3]Nothing is easier than to find fault with any diplomacy (especially papal). Diplomacy, it is well to remember, is the art of the possible. In retrospect, nothing is more tempting than to decry Pius XII for not having made dramatic declarations concerning the wholesale murder of Jews by the Nazis (their other victims ought not be forgotten). The question is not whether it was possible for him to make such declarations, but whether it would it would have been possible for him to achieve thereby anything positive. Interestingly enough, those who nowadays are eager to take to task Pius XII on that score (see, for instance, K. O. von Aretin, *The Papacy and the Modern World*, translated by R. Hill [World University Library; New York: McGraw-Hill, 1970], pp. 225 and 242) are fully satisfied with the policy of accommodation which Paul VI pursues with regimes even more cruel than Nazi Germany and does so with a diplomacy which forever remains the art

of the possible.

[4]*The Letters and Diaries of John Henry Newman*, edited by C. S. Dessain and T. Gornall, vol. XXV (Oxford: Clarendon Press, 1973), p. 137.

[5]The first phrase in P. Gibert, *Les premiers chrétiens découvrent Pierre* (Paris: Desclée de Brouwer/Bellarmin, 1976).

[6]Too many do this to be quoted. What they fail to remember is the statement of Eugene Carson Blake who, as Secretary of the World Council of Churches, noted, in response to the Pope's foregoing phrase, that his candidness had done great service to the cause of Christian unity.

[7]See *Time*'s report (Nov. 14, 1977, pp. 92-93) on the recently published researches of A. B. Hasler on Pius IX and Vatican I.

[8]As claimed in *Council over Pope? Towards a Provisional Ecclesiology* by F. Oakley (New York: Herder and Herder, 1969).

[9]Letter of July 17, 1970, to Edward Husband; see *The Letters and Diaries*, vol. XXV, pp. 160-61.

[10]The Cardinal's conjuring up the tragicomedy of Christian denominations coming closer in points of dogmatic theology but moving apart in points of moral theology, reminded me of the insight the comedian Jackie Gleason displayed on being interviewed in 1961 for a cover story in *Time*. Concerning his reluctance to part with Roman Catholicism which he no longer practiced, Gleason remarked: "Whenever I hear someone say that religion is their own personal affair, I am irritated. Religion can't be called personal. The health of your religion determines the compassion, sympathy, forgiveness, and tolerance you give to your fellow man. I have studied different religions to see if there was one more attractive for me. I only discovered I was seeking a religion that was more compatible to my way of thinking. I remained a Catholic. It wasn't comfortable, but what religion is to a sinner? While I might not carry out my obligations in any manner to be commended, at least I know where I stand." *Time*, Dec. 29, 1961, p. 34.

[11]For its manifestation on the theological level, see, for instance, C. E. Curran and others *Dissent in and for the Church* (New York: Sheed and Ward, 1969).

[12]A good example of this is the short story, "Roman Ordinary," by John L'Heureux in *Harper's* (March, 1977, pp. 38-41), a story remarkable for its grossly bad taste.

[13]*Saint Joan: A Chronicle Play in Six Scenes and an Epilogue* (New York: Dodd, 1926), p. xlix.

[14]The scene was the Sistine Chapel, the date June 27, 1977. "I beg

you on my knees," were Pope Paul's words—words impressing even some news media notoriously hostile to him—to leaders of the Red Brigade imploring them to release the Italian statesman, Aldo Moro.

[15]August 27-September 2, 1977, p. 23.

[16]London: The Bodley Head, 1950, pp. 60-61.

[17]As to ecclesiastical policy, Saint Augustine had already annihilated, on biblical grounds, that strategy as he declared: "There is nothing more serious than the sacrilege of schism because there is no just cause for severing [the] unity [of the Church]" (*non esse quidquam gravius sacrilegio schismatis, quia praecidendae unitatis nulla est justa necessitas*). He warned the self-righteous in the same breath of the simultaneous growth of cockles and wheat. This in turn implied that one, however righteous, had the right to separate himself only from unrighteousness, because severing one's ties with the unrighteous involved separation from the truly righteous. See Augustine's *Contra epistolam Parmeniani*, lib. II, cap. XI, in Migne, *Patrologia Latina*, vol. 43, col. 69.

[18]From J. M. Lloyd Thomas' review of *Enthusiasm* by R. Knox in *The Hibbert Journal* 49 (1951), pp. 305-06.

[19]Letter to Paul VI, Sept. 28, 1968; see *Karl Barth. Letters 1961-1968*, edited by J. Fangmeier and H. Stoevesandt, translated and edited by G. W. Bromiley (Grand Rapids, Michigan: W. B. Eerdmans, 1981), p. 314. Barth praised the "excellent intention of the Holy Father regarding the true relation between marriage and parenthood" in his letter of November 28, 1968, to Cardinal Cicognani. See ibid., p. 335.

[20]Küng was in fact chastised by none other than Karl Barth for his silence on the church in a book dealing with ecclesial veracity. See Barth's letter of October 12, 1968, to Küng, ibid., p. 318.

[21]While the disclosure, on Sept. 28, 1981, in the *Chicago Lawyer*, of tapes on which Fr. Andrew Greeley recorded some of his conversations and ideas to that effect, was unauthorized, it was certainly very revealing of a reforming zeal which is not too evangelical.

V. Divine Origin of the Papacy

The year 1978 was aptly called "the year of three popes," the title of one of the many books recently published on the papacy. The marked increase of publications on a specific topic, like that of the papacy, is a sign of the times. Equally characteristic of our times is the remark which brought that book on the three popes to a close. There its author urged that of the various churches that church will prove to be the most Christian which yields the most for the sake of unity. Such would have been a most wonderful and Christian precept, had it not been left extremely vague and, in all likelihood, deliberately so.

Another theological writer, who hastened to take advantage of a ready market with a book on "the election of the pope," airily remarked before the second papal election of 1978 that, if the new pope smiled and laughed much, it mattered not who or what he was. While such flippancy still keeps asserting itself, the heyday of vagueness as a vehicle for misguided ecumenism is now over. The reason is obvious. The year 1979 turned out to be the year of the pope. Theological writers of a certain type no longer smile while being called, one by one, to explain their voluminous publications through which they aimed at shaping the faith of all Christians with an infallibility which they deny to the pope.

The smiling John XXIII used to say half aloud "facciamo

da Papa" (let us act as pope), so as to warn with humbling tact those around him that his good-natured bantering was not to be construed as if he were unmindful of the weight of his office. While those humbly looking for truth from him needed no such warning, it remained largely ineffective with those who sought above all to promote their own ideas. Indeed, they took his gentle warning as an encouragement to grow bolder. They did the same when confronted with that limitless mercy and patience which were the special characteristics of Paul VI. How the contagious smile of John Paul I would have been abused by these theological writers should be easy to guess. In the long run they would have, however, found a steely resolve beneath that smile. It is well to recall that already at the start of his painfully brief pontificate, John Paul I made it very clear to a large gathering of American bishops that he did not expect fundamental matters, such as the indissolubility of marriage, to be handled with the accommodating smile of worldly wisdom.

All Vaticanologists agree that had the reign of John Paul I not been so short, his successor would not have been the first non-Italian since Adrian VI. The latter, a learned, humble, and saintly Dutch theologian—a combination so rare nowadays—soon found out that humility is only effective with the humble. His great letter, in which he called for reforming the head first if the members of the body were also to be reformed, was turned into inflammatory propaganda material by those who took revolt against authority—a procedure never counseled in the Gospel—as a vehicle of reformation. Revolt against John Paul II, whose election seemed providential even to those Catholics who give more allegiance to the spirit of the times than to the Holy Spirit, quickly began to hatch. Such is more than human logic. The providential role of the pope from Poland will, as should the role of any pope, include the role of that divine sign which is contradicted.

No less quickly, John Paul II proved the year 1979 to be the year of the pope, though not so much through the global excitement that accompanied his visits to Mexico, Poland, and the United States. He is far more than a superstar. Journalists, who feed on excitement, missed the essential in him from the very start. When, in his first public allocution in the Sistine Chapel, he pledged himself to the implementation of Vatican II, the media saw this as a liberal straw in the wind. But while journalists and their theologian ghost-writers had in mind a vague tone of thought to which Vatican II had successfully been degraded in the public mind through the sustained efforts of some *periti* of the Council, the pope had in mind the official documents and decrees of Vatican II. Most of those documents deal with practical matters and they certainly manifest an innovative, creative spirit with which liberalism loves to identify itself. But there is no trace of liberalism, in the sense of vagueness and subjectivism, anywhere in the doctrinal parts of those documents. To see it otherwise demands an unusual degree of wishful thinking, which is, of course, a common characteristic of many a liberal, whether political or ecclesiastical.

The infallibility of Peter and of his successors, which is repeatedly and emphatically stated in the documents of Vatican II, is certainly a startling feature of the system of Catholic dogma. It is, however, no more startling than any dogma properly so called. In any age which admits only opinions but not truth, any dogma will appear startling, and especially one which is tied to a specific human being, the pope. Whether papal infallibility is of divine origin is a question that can be approached in various perspectives. In one chapter, full justice cannot be done even to one such perspective, the infallibility of the extraordinary magisterium of the pope.

Papal infallibility is not a magic power whereby our ordinary human condition is raised to such an extraordinary level that everything becomes absolutely clear, that is, free of any grey area. Revelation leaves essentially intact that human condition which, to paraphrase Paul's words, is to see through a glass darkly. In certain kinds of politics, philosophy, and science which frown upon revelation, the accent all too readily shifts from imperfect seeing to a scepticism void of any vision. This fateful process is precisely what is prevented through a reliance on the light of Revelation. That light secures confidence in trusting our perception of the supernatural as well as of the natural. To keep that light distinct from the mirage of illusions, however sophisticated and fashionable, is the function of an authoritative Magisterium in which the papacy has an irreducible role, both ordinary and extraordinary. Those mindful of the human condition will not find it surprising that even with respect to the pope's extraordinary Magisterium, one shall never have the absolute clarity of mathematical logic, which is a superb tautology anyway. The specification of what amounts to the pope's ordinary Magisterium may cause on occasion even more perplexity. But concerning the moral and doctrinal issues which most agitate our modern society bent on equalizing and liberalizing anything and everybody, John Paul II and his immediate predecessors spoke all too clearly. To be sure, John Paul II did not wish to exercise his extraordinary Magisterium as he prefaced with the words, "I came here as Peter's successor," his quietly firm endorsement, made in Washington, of the practice of admitting only men to the priesthood, a practice as old as the church and as deep as the divine instruction that we should pray to God as our Father who loved the world so much as to send His only begotten Son. (Although He challenged the society of His times and societies of all times in more than one fundamental way, Jesus never did so much as hint that father was interchangeable with mother, or son with daughter.) To dismiss the pope's endorsement of that practice as a mere "allocution," different from "official pronouncements," is an irresponsible play with words. But so is filibuster which no dictionary lists as a synonym for dialogue. Dialogue is not debate, let alone filibuster. Even in political life only those engage in filibuster who know deep in their heart that they shall not prevail. Nor shall the jaws of hell.

For a century or so, the papacy has been officially synonymous with infallibility. Infallibility is a feature whose origin
can hardly be looked for in the human landscape, all too well
known for its countless pitfalls. In this very fallible human
world of ours, nothing in fact can convey with more brute force
the supposedly divine origin of an institution than its claim to
infallibility. When infallibility is grafted on a mere human, such
as the pope, it must therefore be of divine origin. By the same
token there can be no meaningful talk of infallibility if there is
nothing truly divine above the human realm. Those who a century ago took that latter view could only conclude that since the
Papal Realms or States were all too human, the end of the political power of the popes meant the end of the papacy itself.

Speculations about the imminent end of the papacy were
indeed the rage of the day after Garibaldi's troops put an end to
the Papal States. Particularly eager in this respect was Ernest
Renan. During the 1870's and even a little beyond, he repeatedly argued both in print and speeches[1] that the papacy was in
its death throes, a condition marked by feverish and desperate
moves. One such move was, according to Renan, the declaration
of infallibility, a move to forestall, or at least compensate for,
the loss of political power.

Another move, which Renan believed to have been in the
making, was the choice as his successor by Pius IX of a cardinal
with convictions no less extremist than his own. Following the
death of Pius IX, this choice of his would be formally elected
from what Renan called the fanatical faction of the Sacred
College, a faction under the control of the Jesuits. The new
pope would then be quickly expelled from Rome and Italy by
the Italian government. This, in turn, would be followed by the
election of an anti-Pope acceptable both to the government and
to the moderate faction of the Sacred College. Pope and Anti-
pope would then hurl anathemas at each other leading to the
quick disintegration of the papacy as well as of the Catholic
Church.

The quick demise of papacy and Church, as prophesied by Renan, need not detain us. Other parts of Renan's prophesying will appear in their true merit to those who still remember the confident prediction of some theological writers who expected a long and bitterly fought conclave after the death of Paul VI and even more so after the death of John Paul I. Both conclaves should have become such because of an allegedly deep gap between two parties in the Sacred College, a gap stretching all across the Church: hierarchy, clergy, and laity alike. Although those writers labeled the two parties as progressive and conservative, they meant essentially the categories of Renan, that is, moderates and fanatics. Although the prediction of those writers was much more modest in scope than Renan's prophecy, the startling brevity of both conclaves proved them just as wrong as Renan was refuted by what followed the death of Pius IX. The election of Leo XIII was not only not engineered by Pius IX, but also signalled the beginning of an era during which the influence of the papacy and the cohesion of the Church witnessed a steady and almost spectacular growth. Renan, who had cast his lot with a radical form of naturalism, stuck to his perspective. He went on saying, though with gradually decreasing enthusiasm, that God, or the divine, will be organized, that is, explained by science: *"la science organisera Dieu."* He meant by that phrase that historical scholarship (he took the critical investigation of ancient texts, including the Bible, for as high a form of science as were the so-called exact sciences) had shown that God, dogmas, Revelation, and Church are all products of a craving of human nature for something absolutely stable in the welter of change. About such craving Renan would say that it was "fanatical" and that most of mankind would never be cured of it, progress and science notwithstanding.

The bishops, theologians, and laymen who urged and welcomed the declaration of infallibility were seen by Renan as representatives of that craving for at least a minimum of stability. Indeed, though not all of them were minimalists, they came up in the end on the pope's extraordinary magisterium with a decree which is a classic in minimalism. According to that decree the pope is infallible *only* in matters of faith and morals; *only* when he speaks *ex cathedra*; and *only* the very core of his solemn utterance is within the range of his infallibility. The infallibility of the pope does not extend to the explanation of his solemn utterance, not even to its major proofs, be they from the Scriptures, and be they removed but a few lines from the infallible utterance itself.

There is, in fact, a separation of only a few lines between the solemn definition of the universal primacy of Peter perpetuated in the papacy and three scriptural passages, all too well known to be recited in full. They contain respectively the words: "And on this Rock . . ." "Feed my sheep, . . ." and "I prayed for you Simon." These words support in that definition also the infallibility of Peter and of his successors. Primacy and infallibility as understood by Vatican I are but two sides of the same coin and as such they rest on the same foundation.

At this point, and in this age of biblical revival, nothing would be more tempting than to say "biblical foundation" instead of "foundation." But by doing so, one would head into a blind alley, historically as well as biblically. Historically, the Church, both the Church of the Old and of the New Covenant, existed before their Holy Scriptures came into existence. As to the Bible, its witness is very clear about the priority and primacy of the Church over Holy Writ. To be sure, the Scriptures are divinely inspired codification of the authoritative self-reflection of the apostolic Church and they function as permanent norms for a similar reflection in the post-apostolic Church. Anything that contradicts Scriptures cannot be regarded as part of the *depositum fidei*.

The dogma of infallibility is not only not contrary to the Scriptures, but once it is rejected in the name of the Scriptures, there remains no consistent basis for vindicating infallibility for the Scriptures themselves. In our times, a classic illustration of the inner logic of this interconnection was provided in the book *Infallible?*, a book whose author stated that not even the propositions of the Scriptures are strictly inerrant.[2] A very remarkable statement worthy of a great theologian, insofar as the class of great theologians or of philosophers includes not only those who incisively articulate perennial truths, but also who spell out with impressive consistency the ultimate, self-defeating implications of their wrong presuppositions.

Papal infallibility has its own presuppositions, and of these the most important was spelled out by Vatican I, according to which the pope is infallible in the sense in which the Church is infallible. More particularly, papal infallibility is the most specific, tangible aspect of a much broader infallibility which is indeed as broad as is the scope of God's plan of salvation, a plan destined for unfailing, infallible realization. In other words, the infallibility of the divine plan of salvation means, to recall a famous theme of Newman, lasting faithfulness to type.[3] It is a single plan destined to a single fulfillment without ever losing its identity, a plan with a stability strong enough to resist the ever-threatening danger of deformation to which all human endeavors are invariably subject.

Can such a stability be any less than divine? That it is indeed divine has many indications in the Scriptures. It is enough to think of Yahweh's repeated oaths about his living up to his promises, or to think of our Lord's words: "Do not be afraid, I have overcome the world," and "I will be with you until the consummation of the world." Is not unfailing divine stability conveyed in God's promise to Abraham that his descendants will be as numerous as the stars in the sky? Is not the unfailing stability of the Kingdom of God promised in the parable which tells of the full growth of the seed in spite of the enemy's success of sowing cockles under the cover of night?

Such is certainly an unfailing, superhuman, and therefore divine stability, but as the parable states, it does not imply exemption from trying moments and times. Unfailing stability is not uninterrupted sunshine. It is not incompatible with the repeated onset of the dark cover of night during which all our endurance and patience are put to the test. Abraham was tested in many ways, one of them being a trance followed by a deep terrifying darkness. The endurance of the Apostles, and of all their successors and disciples, was put to a perennial test by the warning which forbade them to rush into the field and root up the weeds. Worse, Scriptures tell us that the stability of God's plan can at times weaken almost to the vanishing point. Biblical history is full of such times. There were forty years to be passed in the desert, hardly a symbol of proverbially good stable times. No stretch of imagination can qualify as stable those times which saw the Ark of the Covenant fall into the hands of the Philistines. And what about the times which witnessed the idols of Solomon's concubines (he had a thousand of them) being worshiped in the shadow of the freshly built Temple? Or was there stability, that is, faithfulness to type, during post-Solomonic times, when the northern tribes openly chose schism and to some extent idolatry, and when the south, or Juda, was without Torah and feasts for much of the sixty-year reign of Manasseh?

These ever recurring phases of instability, or apparent fallibility, are an integral part of the New Covenant as well, superior as it is to the Old. The opening phase of its history, as recorded in the *Acts of the Apostles*, is full of moments of instability. In addition to regularly recurring persecutions, there were also vacillations in major policy matters. Peter's opportunist stance on circumcision was challenged by Paul, who later bade Timothy to be circumcised for a similar opportunism, however noble in its scope. Clearly, although the *Acts of the Apostles* is a continual jubilation over God's unfailing plan, it also gives ever-fresh glimpses of how fallible at times can be the actions of this or that Apostle. The freshly founded churches, these outstandingly apostolic acts, provide us with a similar picture. Of the seven churches of Asia, only one is found infallibly faithful to type, namely, to the ideal of a Christian community. Worse, the brief history of those seven churches is an anticipation of a history which more than any other history is bound to remain apocalyptic in the most fearful sense of that word.

The pattern of that history is the darkness of instability dimming the light of stability. To cope with that pattern a continual recourse to God is clearly indispensable. Of that recourse there are many telling examples both in the Old and the New Testament, but perhaps the most graphic and persistent of them is the turning to God as the sole Rock of safety.[4] The image was born out of the landscape, but articulated under divine inspiration and at crucial junctures. God as the Rock is the great recurring theme in the farewell address of Moses, who like all departing leaders was gravely concerned for the stability of what had been established.

Among Moses' legacies were what would now be called responsorial verses, so many exclamations to Yahweh, the sole rock of safety and stability. These verses were so many seeds for future psalms which were constantly on the lips of the people. Indeed, if there was anything to which the people of the Old Testament had often made recourse, it was the utterance that Yahweh was the Rock, the sole Rock of stability, refuge of safety, assurance of permanence, that is, of faithfulness to type. The Old Testament had its series of great heroes and saints, who acted like stability incarnate, but none of them was called rock, let alone given the name Rock, although the giving of descriptive names was not at all rare among the Jews. Indeed, Jesus was Jewish enough to call James and John *"Boanerges"* (Sons of Thunder), for their readiness to call fire from Heaven upon some unfriendly villages. The name, being a momentary reproof, did not stick. What a contrast with Jesus calling Simon the Rock (*Cephas,* Peter) at their very first meeting! Of course, Jesus used the word *kepha*, a synonym for *sur*, because the latter was part of the hallowed expression, Yahweh the Rock (*Yah-sur*). Had Jesus called Simon not *kepha* but *sur*, those around

Him would have sensed blasphemy. But the word *kepha* was close enough in meaning to *sur* to let everybody realize its importance as a name for Simon.

A year or so later, Simon was declared to be the Rock itself. The phrasing was so unmistakably Aramaic as to exclude the possibility of later forgery. The scenery of the words, "And on this Rock," is somewhat conjectural, though worth exploring.[5] The huge wall of rock over the source of the Jordan was visible to anyone "in the neighborhood of Caesarea Philippi." On the top of that rock there glittered Jupiter's temple; below, next to the source of the Jordan, there was a cave, a famous sanctuary of Pan. Jupiter and Pan were the great symbols of state worship and nature worship, the two perennial deadly traps for fallible man. Jesus indeed could hardly have chosen in the entire land a better backdrop for His words that the jaws of Hell shall not prevail over His Church built on Peter, the Rock.

There has been a chronic neglect of that scenery on the part of biblical scholars, so ready to discourse for hours on end about a preposition or to dig up potsherds by the ton. But biblical scholars, like other scholars, are fallible and certainly very much the children of their own times. They should better recall that subjective idiosyncrasies and presuppositions play havoc with scholarship even in those fields, the mathematical and physical sciences, whose methods and objects are far less subjective than is the case with most topics of biblical scholarship or rather criticism, so ready to lay a fundamental claim to objectivity in matters theological.

Such a claim will not overly impress anyone aware of more than the gossip of the moment in any particular field, be it the field of biblical criticism. Should we readily forget that around 1870 cultivators (mostly Protestant) of biblical criticism assured the world that Christ never spoke the words "And on this Rock," or if He did, he meant only faith, perhaps Peter's faith, but certainly not Peter himself? Surely we can be most gratified by the fact that in more recent times, Kittel, Cullmann and many lesser names have come around to admitting that Peter himself was meant by those words. Surely we can be gratified that it is no longer fashionable in biblical scholarship to doubt Peter's leadership among the Twelve. But should we also believe that it was not rational, scholarly, and objective to believe in the primacy of Peter until biblical criticism caught up with the idea in these last days? Would not such subservience to the shifting moods of biblical criticism be a catastrophic prospect for reason as well as faith? After all, biblical criticism, or at least the "accepted" or "in" wing of it still denies us the continuity of Peter's primacy and with it continued infallibility and indefectibility for the Church as well.

No different is the case when one turns to the scholarly evaluation of the record of the first two or three Christian centuries concerning the role of Peter's successors in the Church. The venture may simply be misplaced if too much weight is given to a not-too-old and highly acclaimed book on ecclesiology according to which even a thousand years later, that is, during the High Middle Ages, papal infallibility can be found only in its germ in the record.[6] According to another recent and major monograph, papal infallibility owes its origin to the excessive zeal of some early Franciscan theologians.[7] Clearly, what is then the point of looking for any evidence for infallibility in the first three centuries?

Let us therefore be more modest and go back only as far as the beginning of this century. Then the record in question appeared rather different to Catholic theologians not yet swayed by some Utopian vision of ecumenism or by the subtle strategy of Protestantizing the Church from within, a strategy which Pope Paul VI decried in an agonizing utterance. As to Protestant theologians, hardly any of them could at that time be suspect of an overweening sympathy for Roman Catholicism in their reading of the record. One of the most prominent of them, Harnack, was indeed too much of a liberal to have sympathy for even traditional Protestantism. Thus we may reasonably assume that only respect for the historical record prompted him to write in his famed *History of Dogma* that the first letter of Clement, bishop of Rome, written to the Corinthians, "proves that, by the end of the first century, the Roman Church had already drawn up fixed rules for her own guidance, that she watched with motherly care over outlying communities, and that she then knew how to use language that was at once an expression of duty, love, and authority."[8] Almost exactly a hundred years later there came the famous edict of Victor I, an edict declaring that any local church that failed to conform with Rome was excluded from the union of the one Church on the ground of heresy. Harnack wondered aloud:

> How would Victor have ventured on such an edict— though indeed he had not the power of enforcing it in every case—unless the special prerogative of Rome to determine the conditions of the 'common unity' in the vital questions of faith had been an acknowledged and well established fact? How could Victor have addressed such a demand to the independent churches, if he had not been recognized, in his capacity of bishop of Rome, as the special guardian of the 'common unity'?[9]

The forcefulness of Harnack's words are undeniable but are, therefore, the texts he reflected upon a support of papal infallibility? They are, indeed, as long as one looks for things and not mere words. A historian of the dogma of the Eucharist, who is satisfied with nothing short of the expression 'Real Presence', must wait until the Middle Ages, but then what is he going to do with the words of Saint Augustine, according to whom during the last supper "Christ carried that Body (of His) in His own hands"?[10] Much the same is true about the early record concerning infallibility. It clearly contains the thing, that is, the reality of the infallibility of the Bishop of Rome, though not the expression of itself. But to perceive things beneath the words as far as history is concerned, one must have a notion of history

such as the one formulated by Newman and in that very book
of his which is the record of his agonizing search as to where
"faithfulness to type" is preserved:

> History is not a creed or catechism, it gives lessons rather
> than rules; . . . bold outlines and broad masses of color rise
> out of the records of the past. They may be dim, they may
> be incomplete; but they are definite . . . to be deep in his-
> tory is to cease to be a Protestant.[11]

To such an approach to history it will be objected that it
prejudges history, that it forces one in advance to decide what
to look for in history, to the detriment of a critical scholarship
free of presuppositions. The objection has long been answered
by Newman, who had repeatedly endorsed papal infallibility as
a theological tenet prior to its definition at Vatican I and,
though he viewed that definition inopportune, accepted it un-
reservedly. Its latter-day Roman Catholic critics would do well
to ponder Newman's penetrating observation about objectors to
the dogma of Immaculate Conception: "I have never heard of
one Catholic having difficulty in receiving it, whose faith on
other grounds was not already suspicious."[12]

That scholars, devoted to criticism—biblical, patristic, or of
any kind—would ever start their learned treatises on infallibility with a candid avowal of their really fundamental difficulty
about it, would be indulging in utopistic hopes. There was no
such candidness on the part of the ten drafters of that sad document released in the wake of the death of Paul VI, a document outlining the features of the pope needed by our times.
Tellingly enough, while those ten bravely instructed the future
pope, they were not candid enough to state that the kind of
pope they clamored for was not to instruct the theologians, let
alone to instruct them with the authority of his infallibility.

Whereas to many theologians that document appeared in-
nocuous and noble, a lay contributor to the *Times* (London)
bluntly laid bare its true character. It was branded there as a

"takeover bid which needs to be resisted," simply because "Scripture and tradition both suggest that the role of the theologian within the Church, although important, is secondary." More importantly, the true moral character of that document was also made clear in a remark which really went to the heart of the matter: "We are long accustomed to hearing harsh things said about the dogmatism of popes and prelates. But imagine one man saying 'We know the answers and intend to call the shots, because we are extremely clever people and have studied this matter very thoroughly,' while another man said 'This is the message we were told to pass on to you.' Which of these two would display the greater pride?"[13]

Plain pride hiding behind the facade of learnedness, if not mere cleverness, is a far cry from the attitude of those few, such as Newman, who were great enough, both as persons and scholars, to be utterly candid. This is why Newman's testimony is so precious,[14] especially at a time when some Catholic theologians are turning him, and with impunity, into a champion of liberalism. They certainly disregard—in round indictment of their allegedly critical scholarship—Newman's ringing declaration made in 1879: "For 30, 40, 50 years I have resisted to the best of my powers the spirit of liberalism in religion." Possibly, they keep under cover these words of their hero, or rather stalking horse, because there is too much relevance for present times in those words and their continuation: "Never did the Holy Church need champions against it [liberalism] more sorely than now, when, alas, it is an error overspreading, as a snare, the whole Earth."[15]

Those theologians, almost to a man latter-day modernist critics of papal infallibility, seem to overlook a very curious difference between Newman and themselves. While Newman humbly confessed that he had never sinned against the Holy Spirit, they boldly speak in the name of that Spirit. But as all too often in the past, the step from *Heiliger Geist* (Holy Spirit) to *Zeitgeist* (spirit of times) is a very short step. And what if that spirit is merely the *Geist* to which Hegel paid supreme homage, but which turned out to be his own sadly fallible mind trapped in the labyrinths not so much of its own evolution as of its endless convolutions?

Indeed, much futile debate about infallibility and ecclesiology could be eliminated if a theologian would be honest and courageous enough to start his treatises and manifestos with the naming of his favorite philosopher. And if he claims that he has none, then he should not consider himself qualified for writing theology. Underlying all attacks against infallibility there lies a philosophy whose claims are far less modest than those of Vatican I. This is particularly true of the attacks of modernists, old and new, against papal infallibility. On the face of it, most of them only replace that infallibility with another, say, with that of the Bible, or of Councils—an enterprise that has already many times revealed its self-defeating character. As to the Bible, Luther himself had to fall back on his own infallibility against the Anabaptists who hurled their own readings of the Bible at him. As to the Councils, no less resolute a biblical critic than Bultmann provided a priceless witness not too many years ago. On reading Rahner's rebuttal of Küng's book on infallibility, Bultmann hastened to tell in a letter to Rahner of his agreement and added: "How fortunate you must be to be able to appeal to the Pope; appeal to the Lutheran synods merely leads to greater disunity."[16] In some cases, however, the infallibility of the Pope is replaced neither with that of the Bible or of Councils, but with that of opinion polls in which truth is the hapless victim of the ever-shifting majority. Such a majority belongs to that parliament of religions within whose walls, to recall Chesterton's words, "believers" pay constant homage to "each other's unbelief."[17]

Also, to take a quick look at the non-modernist side, not a few sincere defenders of infallibility would do far better than Rahner, who at the end of his debate with Küng was trapped in a subtly anti-intellectual stance: "I can do nothing else except

contradict Küng's basic thesis once again," a stance which reminded a fence-sitting discussant of infallibility of Luther's famous words: "Here I stand and can do no otherwise."[18] Rahner,
of course, would not have been trapped in a clearly subjective
assertion of the truth, had he really perceived what was truly
basic in Küng's thesis. That basic factor was related not to theology, but to philosophy, or rather epistemology. Could, however,
the truly basic point of epistemology be reached within the bot-
tomless transcendental Thomism professed by Rahner, a
Thomism which is a pathetic, unwitting sellout of the objectivity
and realism of Thomas to the subjective idealism of Kant?[19]

What makes Kant's epistemology so incurably subjective is
that it leaves no logical room for error.[20] A far cry from Aristo-
tle's remark that it is natural for a man to spend much of his
life in error in most things, a remark not frowned upon by
Thomas. Within that epistemological perspective, the exercise of
infallibility as a rare definition or formulation of truth will not
appear something irrational. Papal infallibility does not mean
that erroneous views will cease to be popular among those sub-
mitting to its rare *dicta*. It does not mean that popes themselves
will be daily oracles of truth, or that their countless utterances
should be endlessly scanned as if they were Holy Writ. Papal infallibility does not mean that we should turn into those hotheads
of whom St. Francis de Sales wrote that "since our age is full of
them, it is rather difficult to say something that would not of-
fend those who by making themselves into lackeys of popes and
princes want that one should never stop short of extremes."[21]

What papal infallibility means is that the divine plan of
salvation remains faithful to type in the midst of rapidly
changing fashions of theological and philosophical thought. Papal infallibility means that the Church as a whole never will fail
in the proper knowledge of the Father and of His will, that is,
plan of salvation, a knowledge, which according to Jesus' words,
is salvation itself. Since, however, there is only one salvation, the
kind of knowledge which is salvation must remain one, that is,

faithful to itself across space and especially time. Hence, the plan of salvation must possess a built-in safeguard which, as Bible, Tradition, and history attest, can only be Peter living in his successors. Therefore, papal infallibility implies on the part of all those for whose safeguard it is given, an unswerving adherence to that rock foundation on which alone can rise that Church-edifice within which alone can the paschal meal be eaten in a rightful manner, to recall a warning of St. Jerome, the greatest biblical scholar of all times.[22]

To continue with the Bible, that church-edifice is made up of stones, spiritually living stones, each one of which can at any time turn into a dead, decaying piece. There were in fact popes who as persons were plain harbingers of spiritual decay. Of these incidents much has been made in the past and with a self-righteousness clothed in an apparently biblical indignation. But is it not that indignation which leads time and again to a stance branded unbiblical by our Lord's very words, "he who does not gather with me scatters"? Are not these words of his a warning against an "ecclesial indignation," in which, under the pretext of "gathering," one turns his back on the center, a move which deprives one by the same stroke of the only consistent point of reference? Or to be less philosophical and more biblical: Is it not in the Bible that we find the difference between that son of Noah who made fun of his father's shame and those sons of his who did not even then refuse to respect him?

At that moment there was a painful mixture of heavy darkness and flickering light in Noah's house, an allegory for the Church itself as to what can happen at times within its walls. It may indeed have been Heaven's warning that when on Monday morning, July 18, 1870, the final vote was taken in St. Peter's on infallibility, a storm of unusual violence raged over Rome. By noon, when it came for Pius IX to read out the doctrine *ex cathedra*, the darkness cast by the clouds was so heavy as to restore proper usefulness to the *bugia*, a small ceremonial candle. This detail has often been noted for its symbolic portent by historians of Vatican I.[23] To appreciate it should be rather easy for anyone aware of the true condition of Christians, a condition of pilgrims, of wanderers. In their pursuit of a long faraway goal, nothing would be more dangerous than the illusion that the final destiny is near at hand or that storms during their journey ought to be few and far between. But their worse error would be to deprecate the often meager light available during their journey and not to have their gaze fixed on it. It is a light which may flicker at times, but burn it never fails. Unfailingly faithful to type, it can only be infallible and therefore of divine origin.

NOTES

[1]Details are given in all major accounts of Renan's life and work. For a specially documented account, see L. Vie, *Renan* (Paris: Bloud and Gay, 1949), pp. 495-517.

[2]H. Küng, *Infallible? An Inquiry*, tr. E. Quinn (Garden City: Doubleday, 1971), pp. 219-220.

[3]The "preservation of type" is the first of seven notes distinguishing genuine development from deformation in Newman's *An Essay on the Development of Christian Doctrine* (new ed.; London: Basil Montagu Pickering, 1878), pp. 171-78. The "unity of type" active in the Church is the reason, according to Newman, why she is always decried by her critics as being "incorrigible."

[4]For further details see ch. II.

[5]For photographic and archeological illustrations, see ch. I.

[6]Y. Congar, *L'Eglise de Saint Augustin à l'époque moderne* (Paris: Cerf, 1970), p. 24.

[7]B. Tierney, *Origins of Papal Infallibility, 1150-1350: A Study on the Concepts of Infallibility, Sovereignty and Tradition in the Middle Ages* (Leiden: E.J. Brill, 1972).

[8]A. Harnack, *History of Dogma*, tr. N. Buchanan (2nd ed.; London: Williams and Norgate, 1896), vol. 2, pp. 155-56.

[9]Ibid., p. 161.

[10]*Enarratio in Psalmos* (Ps. 33, I, 10) in Migne, *Patr. Lat.* vol. 36, col. 306.

[11]*An Essay on the Development of Christian Doctrine*, pp. 7-8.

[12]*Apologia pro vita sua* (Garden City: Doubleday, 1956), p. 330.

[13]Christopher Derrick in *Times* (London), Aug. 26, 1978, p. 14, col. 6. That document must have obviously been in the mind of the Editor himself, as he had noted three days earlier: "A Pope who sought to divest himself of Papal authority would fracture the Roman Church without in all likelihood winning the adherence of any other group of Christians" (ibid., Aug. 23, 1978, p. 13).

[14]Gladstone's words on Newman's importance have indeed an eery timeliness: "In my opinion his secession from the Church of England has never yet been estimated among us at anything like the full amount of its calamitous importance. It has been said that the world does not know its greatest men; neither, I will add, is it aware of the power and weight carried by the words and by the acts of those among its greatest men it does know." See G. B. Smith, *The Life of the Right Honorable William Ewart Gladstone* (New York: G. P. Putnam, 1880), p. 499.

[15]From his speech in 1879 on being created a cardinal. The entire speech is given in W. Ward, *Life of John Cardinal Newman* (London: Longmans, Green, 1912), vol. II, pp. 458-62.

[16]Passages from that letter were read by Rahner himself publicly during his visit in England in 1971. See *The Tablet*. March 10, 1979, p. 238, col. 3.

[17]G.K. Chesterton, *A Miscellany of Men* (2nd ed.; London: Methuen, 1912), p. 188. The passage is from the essay, "The New Theologian," with an uncanny relevance for the 1960's and 1970's.

[18]Harry J. McSorley in J. J. Kirvan (ed.), *The Infallibility Debate* (New York: Paulist Press, 1971), p. 95.

[19]This is not the place to discuss the inherent connection between a theologian's epistemology and his views of papal infallibility. A mere recall of salvation as being a knowledge (far more to be sure than mere theorizing, but still knowledge) should indicate the existence of such a connection. No true Thomist is known to have been an opponent, a critic, or a diluter of the idea of papal infallibility. On the other hand, no modernist and liberal theologians have ever been adherents to Thomism. They all follow Ockham into the morass of nominalism whatever the label they put on it.

[20]The ultimate reason for the impossibility of errors in all nonrealist epistemologies is that they leave no logical room for wonderment, the starting point of philosophy. See my Gifford Lectures, *The Road of Science and the Ways to God* (Chicago: University of Chicago Press, 1978, pp. 257-58.

[21]Letter. Nr. 761, in *Oeuvres de Saint-François de Sales* (Lyons: E. Vitte, 1892-1925), vol. 15, p. 192.

[22]See p. 94

[23]See T.G. Jalland, *The Church and the Papacy* (London: S. P. C. K., 1944), p. 11.

Chapel in honor of Saint Peter on a hilltop south of the wall of rock, a casualty of the war of 1967 (photograph by the author, 1976)

Epilogue

in the form of a formula for complaint
to those bent on complaining
about the Rock, the Pope:

"Take care that I do not have to complain about you to Jesus crucified. There is no one else I can complain to, for you have no superior on earth."

> Saint Catherine of Siena
> *in a letter to*
> *Pope Gregory XI (1340-78),*
> *who owing to her humble and holy pleas*
> *reluctantly left Avignon for Rome—*
> *ending thereby the Babylonian captivity*
> *of the papacy.*

May not that crucified Jesus have to complain to his heavenly Father about us complaining disciples.